FIXED HEAD COUPÉ

PRINCIPAL DIMENSIONS: Wheelbase, 8 ft. 0 ins.; Track, front and rear, 4 ft. 2 ins.; Overall length, 14 ft. 7 5/16 ins.; Overall width, 5 ft. 5 1/4 ins.; Overall height, 4 ft. 0 ins.; Ground clearance (laden), 5 1/2 ins.; Turning circle 37 ft.; Fuel tank capacity 14 imp. gallons.

JAGUAR

race...Space...Pace

2 + 2 MODEL

ROADSTER

The Jaguar XK-E Roadster is a beautiful two-seater sports car. It is also much more than that. It is five great victories at Le Mans. It is country living in the city. It is Briggs Cunningham, Walt Hansgen and Alfred Momo. It is the sparkle of 72-spoke chromed wire wheels spinning down Wilshire Boulevard. And it is a speedometer that reads to 160 mph because it has to.

Some XK-E Roadster features are classic, unchangeable. Such is the svelte, wind-formed shape, with the louvered hood hinging upward for total access to the aluminum-head twin-camshaft engine, tamed from racing for your enjoyment on the road. And there could be no replacement for the form-fitting reclining seats, mance, all of which are the hallmarks of this, the world's most outstanding G.T. car. The 4.2 litre 'XK' engine is fitted as standard to all 'E' type models and provides outstanding acceleration and flexibility of performance throughout its very wide speed range. Each model features rich upholstery, fitted carpets, extensive safety padding, comprehensive instrumentation and fresh air heating and ventilation. Each model combines outstanding handling with the luxury of saloon car comfort — a special kind of motoring which no other car in the world can offer.

NEW EFFORTLESS BRAKING New brake servo gives lower effort and greater power for the disc brakes on all four wheels. Separate fluid systems for front and rear give added safety.

ALTERNATOR gives greatly increased current supply over wide range of engine speeds, ensuring adequate current supply—even with city driving—for the extensive electrical service embodied.

PRE-ENGAGED STARTER facilitates starting under conditions of extreme cold.

SHAPED SEATING designed for maximum comfort, and upholstered in finest quality Vaumol leather over Dunlopillo foam rubber cushions.

ENGINE
...inder, twin overhead cam-design of race-proved 3...uar XK engine, five times ...ans, gives higher torque for ...eration and flexibility.

...SH GEARBOX
...synchro crash-proof trans-...smooth, rapid changes. ...ng clutch gives lighter pedal ...g life.

...ING
...s lower effort and greater ...e brakes on all four wheels. ...stems for front and rear

JAGUAR
Grace...Space...Pace

JAGUAR XK-E

CELEBRATING THE JAGUAR E-TYPE **50** FIFTY YEARS OF A DESIGN ICON

WWW.JAGUAR.COM

THE TABLE OF CONTENTS

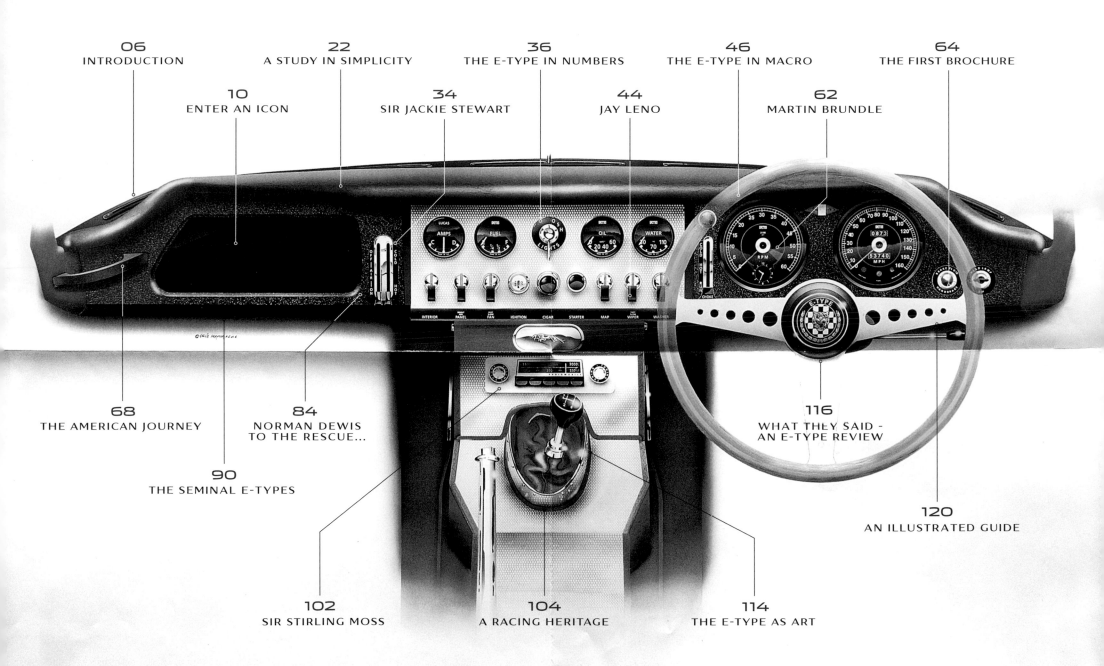

E-TYPE JAGUAR
Jaguar – 'A dash of elegance' series: No.2

Sir William Lyons, Chairman and Managing Director
of Jaguar Cars Limited and Mr. W. M. Heynes
Chief Engineer, request the pleasure of the company
of _____
at a press conference to introduce the new Jaguar Type 'E'
on Wednesday the 15th of March 1961 at 4.30 P.M.
at the restaurant du Parc des Eaux Vives in Geneva

R.S.V.P. to Jaguar Information Service
3, Saint Pierre, Lausanne   *Personal*
Tel. (021) 22 76 78

"DRIVING SHOULD BE A JOY, NOT A CHORE"

SIR WILLIAM LYONS, FOUNDER, JAGUAR CARS

Every great company has a product that instantly elevates it head and shoulders above the competition. At Jaguar we are very fortunate to have had not just one but many such stars throughout our history.

However, if one car could be said to be not merely a halo product but a hero, it is the E-Type. This is a car that not only embodied the true meaning behind Sir William Lyons' words – the beauty, speed and innovation of a sports car – but also captured the revolutionary spirit of an entire era.

Having created a car of such iconic stature serves as a daily reminder of the responsibility for everyone at Jaguar to carry forward the proud traditions of the company.

Now the world has moved on – the E-Type can never, and should never, be recreated. But at Jaguar we work every single day to leave the world with beautiful, fast cars that will inspire similar passions half a century from now.

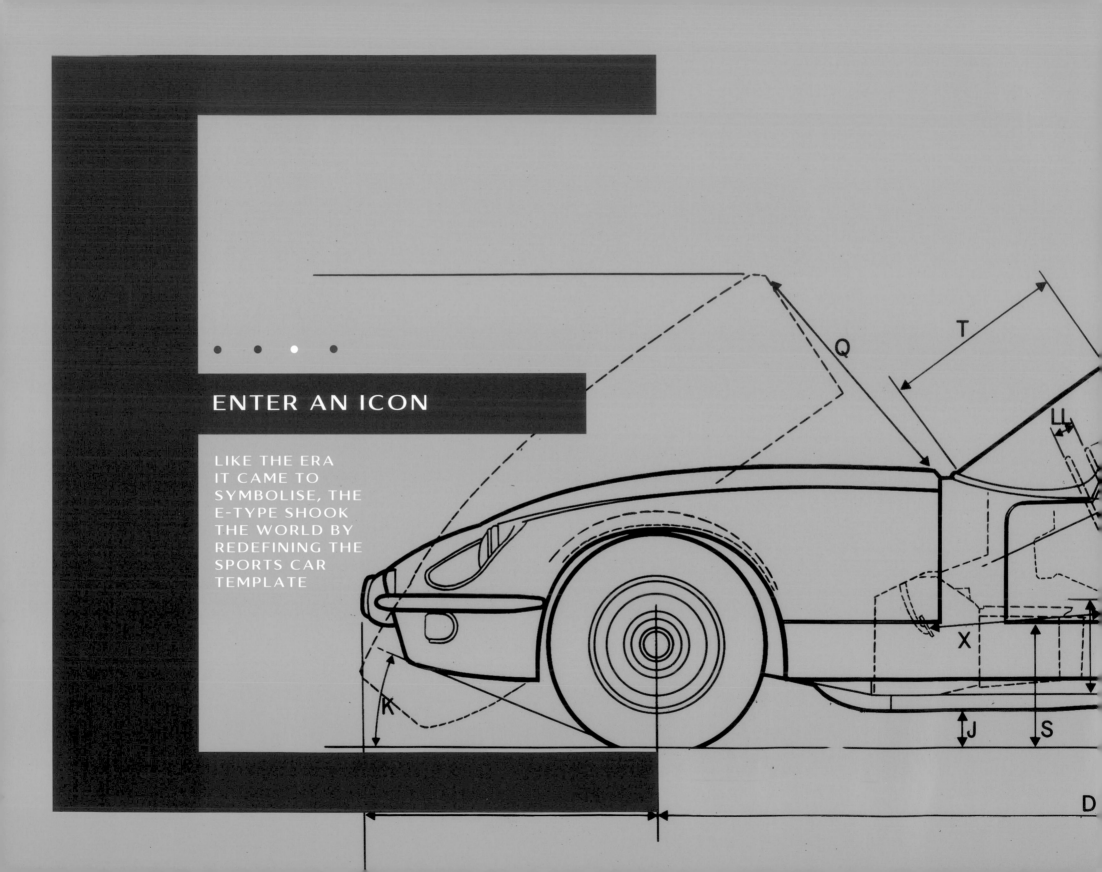

ENTER AN ICON

LIKE THE ERA
IT CAME TO
SYMBOLISE, THE
E-TYPE SHOOK
THE WORLD BY
REDEFINING THE
SPORTS CAR
TEMPLATE

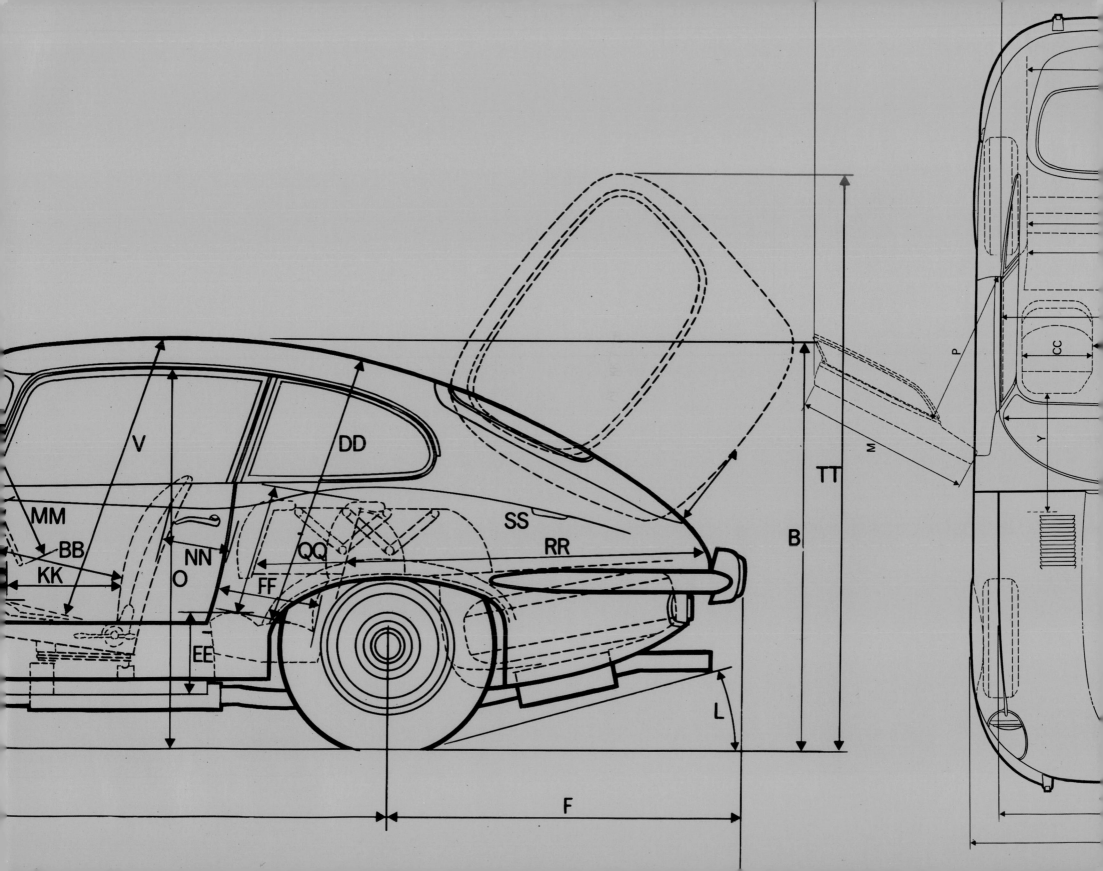

THE E1A PROTOTYPE Was the steam roller a subtle allusion to the advances about to be made?

The 1960s was a decade defined by icons and heroes and 1961 had more than its fair share. There was Yuri, the first man to leave the confines of our planet. There was John, the American President who accepted the Soviet challenge and committed his country to sending Neil, Buzz and Michael to the Moon.

In California, Brian, Dennis, Carl, Mike and Al became better known as The Beach Boys. Meanwhile, in Liverpool, John, Paul, George and Ringo played their first gig at the Cavern Club. Then, just a month after the Beatles took to the stage for the first time, William, Bill, Malcolm and Norman unveiled the car that came to embody the spirit of the age.

The decade that became known as the Swinging Sixties was a time of revolution, liberation, innovation, socialisation and, of course, sexualisation. The E-Type encapsulated all of those things. It was the world's fastest production car, capable of 150mph yet tractable and comfortable enough not to be the preserve of the unenlightened male. Its styling, by aerodynamicist Malcolm Sayer, was the epitome of grace, appreciated by both sexes at a time when the struggle for equality entered its fiercest stage. And it was no unattainable supercar but a reliable and, above all, affordable sports car.

The E-Type's development actually began in the preceding decade as Jaguar founder Sir William Lyons looked to replace the XK sports car, which had itself been crowned world's fastest production car in 1948. The intervening years had seen Jaguar dominant on the racetrack, particularly at the 24 Hours of Le Mans, with the C and D-Type racers, and it was the lessons learnt from these cars that would inform the design of the E-Type – as well as giving it a name.

THE E-TYPE WAS NO UNATTAINABLE SUPERCAR BUT A RELIABLE AND AFFORDABLE SPORTS CAR

The first prototype, E1A, was completed in 1957. Built from aluminium, it utilised a central monocoque and exotic magnesium framework to support the 2.4–litre straight–six, an engine design masterminded by chief engineer Bill Heynes. The main purpose of the car was to test the firm's all–independent rear suspension which, as designed by engineer Bob Knight, would underpin Jaguars for years to come and create a legendary reputation for ride comfort.

As the new decade dawned and Elvis Presley returned to the United States from a stint of military service in Europe, another American, Briggs Cunningham was heading in the other direction. The racing fanatic had seen the second E–Type development car, E2A, and persuaded Jaguar that the new design should be evaluated in the heat of competition. Although this car shared much with the earlier racers, such as its D–Type tailfin, its overall lines marked it out as a forebear to the E–Type. With steel bodywork over an aluminium chassis and 3.0–litre engine, E2A set the fastest lap at Le Mans and ran as high as third before retiring.

FRANK SINATRA IS REPUTED TO HAVE SAID: 'I WANT THAT CAR AND I WANT IT NOW...'

All this was forgotten, however, at 4.30pm on March 15th 1961, when the roadgoing E–Type was unveiled in Geneva. The reaction was nothing short of astonishing, with so many people clamouring to be given demonstration rides that local police had to be brought in to keep order. Jaguar took 500 orders at the show and when, a month later, the car was displayed in New York, Frank Sinatra is reputed to have said: "I want that car and I want it now..."

The key was not merely the E–Type's performance, although with a 265bhp, triple–carburetted, 3.8–litre version of the straight–six, there was no shortage of that, but the price at which Jaguar was able to offer it. A new E–Type was half the price of an Aston Martin or Ferrari, none of which could match its record–breaking speed.

A DAY AT THE RACES The second prototype, E2A, became a familiar sight on the track

BRITISH BEAUTY It's not hard to see why the E-Type is perhaps the most elegant car ever made

Plaudits galore were heaped upon the E-Type and it soon attracted a pantheon of famous owners including George Best, Britt Ekland and George Harrison. However the Jaguar ethos has always been one of continuous refinement and changes were not long in coming. As the Beatles kicked off the 'British Invasion' of the USA with a 1964 appearance on the Ed Sullivan Show, the E-Type was changing in response to demands from its biggest market. The engine grew in size to 4.2 litres, with a commensurate torque increase, while the Moss gearbox was pensioned off to be replaced with an all-synchromesh unit.

It was the American journalist Henry Manney that dubbed the E-Type the "greatest crumpet-catcher known to man" and in 1966 Jaguar launched the variant that addressed the needs of the man whose crumpet-catching had resulted in the pitter-patter of tiny feet: the family-friendly 2+2. In 1967, the headlight covers were removed to comply with new US safety regulations and the following year, further changes created the Series 2, which featured a larger air intake to cope with the cooling demands of power steering and air conditioning.

It may now be hard to believe but by the start of the 1970s, the E-Type had lost some of its lustre and Jaguar decided to do something radical by entering the decade with a new powerplant. Intended for the XJ12 saloon, the E-Type was a perfect home for the new 5.3-litre V12. To accommodate the larger engine the 2+2 chassis was standardised and a larger grille and flared wheel-arches distinguished the new Series 3 from earlier E-Types. However, propitious as the original E-Type's timing may have been, the Series 3 was not so lucky, global events conspiring against it. The 1973 oil crisis made large-capacity engines less desirable and E-Type production was ended early, in 1974, before its XJ-S replacement was even ready...

E-TYPE ATTRACTED A PANTHEON OF FAMOUS OWNERS FROM GEORGE BEST TO GEORGE HARRISON

BODY BUILDING E-Types roll down the production line at Jaguar's Browns Lane factory

THE BOOK
OF RECORDS

It's slightly dog-eared now, but this bound volume is a treasure trove of information for E-Type owners and enthusiasts the world over. Held safely in the archives of the Jaguar Heritage Trust it is one of seven containing data on every E-Type to leave the factory. From the chassis numbers, to the engine specifications, colours and even names of the first owner, every entry was recorded by hand.

CHASSIS COMPLETED	CHASSIS No.	ENGINE No.	HORSE POWER	BODY TYPE	CARD No.	BODY No.	COLOUR	DISTRIBUTOR	DATE OF INVOICE	INVOICE No.	CREDITS, IF ANY	KEYS I	KEYS B	PETROL	DATE OF DESPATCH	GUARANTEE DATE AND OWNER	REMARKS
7.66	1E50261	7E51500-9	4.2	FHC	4E	51628	Ch.Lt. Maroon/Maroon	Jag. Dist. 808	19.7.66	78418	TSC 2962	902	885	8	15.7.66	MR Watnough. WS Manor Heath East Morton Keighley Yorks	MWU 986 D Jowett MTS 19 7 66
	EJ 14667	F	SN 6322/41			B 15/7											
	1E50262	7E51493-9	F66 179			51630	Dark Blue/Lt. Blue	Hatfield 5834	20.7.66	75998 CEH7287		902	885	7	15.7.66	Altonite Refractories 543? Ecclesall Rd Sheffield 11	1 CWB Retail 20 7 66
	EJS. 8899	F	S66 2491 SN 6322/41			B 15/7											
	1E50263	7E51458-9	G66 2483			51633	Silver Grey/Red	Bellamy 144	19.7.66	74982	TSC 2959	902	885	8	15.7.66	MR D G Stevens Tregarthen Hse Sibsey Nr Boston Lincs	GEE 479 D Retail 20 9 66
	EJS. 8773	G — F	6322/41			B 15/7											
	1E50364	7E51558-9	G66 2489			51635	Silver Grey/Red	Henlys L. 3527	23.3.67	78201	TSC 4918 2928	902	885	8	20.7.66	J E Cole Esq 22 Lower Rd Fetcham Leatherhead Sy	PPH 525 E H W Motors Ltd 1 3 67
	EJ 9631	H	6322/41			B 15/7											
7.66	1E50265	7E51543-9	G66 2478			51637	Silver Blue/D. Blue	Mortons D87	20.7.66	76053	TSC 2963	902	885	8	15.7.66	MR OLAF Jones The Oaklands Bridgend Glam	KTX 991 D Retail 20 7 66
	EJS. 9448	G	6322/41			B 15/7											
	1E50266	7E51630-9	G66-2490 - 43/1494			51632	Dark Blue/Lt. Blue	Henlys L. 3520	8.3.67	78194	TSC 4788	902	885	8	22.8.66	Sherman Morgan Ltd Albion Works Sigdon Rd E8	NYM 165 E MP HA Fox Co Ltd 24.2.67
	EJS 8901	G	SN 6322/41			B 15/7											
	1E50267	7E51635-9	G66 2481			51641	Silver Blue/Grey	Henlys L. 3516	14.10.66	78190	TSC 3771	902	885	8	19.7.66	MAJ. Smith Esq 5, Brecon Close Swindon Wilts.	N. PG. 858D. Coombes & Sons Ltd, Goldsh 10.8.66
	EJS. 8668	G	SN 6322/41			B 15/7											
	1E50268	7E51631-9	G66 2477			51640	Silver Blue/D. Blue	Crosston Preston 1554	20.7.66	74974	TSC 2958	902	885	1	18.7.66	MR S Burridge 206 Lord St Fleetwood Lancs	BTF 840 E Jag Centre 21.3.67
	EJS 9545	HHHHSH	SN 6322/41			B 15/7											
	1E50269	7E51446-8	C66-1036			51570	Primrose/Black	Henlys 63968 Mr. G. Farkas	5.8.66	63968	3945 2856	902	885	—	3.8.66		HWK 422 D
	EJ 10836	H — GHG	SN 6322/27			B 15/7											
	1E50270	7E51611-9	G66 2503			51634	Silver Grey/Red	P.G. Evans 1723	10.2.67	75925	TSC 4683	902	885	4	2.8.66	Monarch Roofing Co Audham Stourbridge Works	NUY 696 E Stanley Goodwin
	EJS 2470		SN 6322-41			B 5/8											
	1E50271	7E51645-9	G66 2499			51618	Cream/D. Blue	Henlys L. 3518	24.2.67	78192	TSC 4753	902	855	8	29.7.66	Wholesale Textile Co, Cambridge Ltd York Terrace, Cambridge	GCE 891 E Hurketts Bros 2 2 67
	EJS 9748		SN 6322-41			B 15/7											
	1E50272	7E51623-9	G66 2507			51644	Sherwood/S.Green	Henlys L. 3514	20.7.66	78188	TSC 2851	902	895	8	18.7.66	N E Hill Esq Sunnybrooke House Andoversford Cheltenham Glos	JAD 661 D Imperial MTS Chelten 3 9 66
	EJS 9614	H	SN 6322/41			B 15/7											
	1E50273	7E51567-9	G66 2512			51636	Silver Blue/D. Blue	Henlys L. 3511	20.7.66	78185	TSC 3006	885	885	8	18.7.66	Fw Belcher - Son 30 Blackmore Lane Maidenhead Berks	LBL 900 E Great Western MTS 2 1 67
	EJS 9541	PG'999	SN 6322/41			B 15/7											
	1E50274	7E51652-9	G66-2498			51646	Sherwood/S.Green	Henlys L. 3529	12.9.66	78203	3448	885	885	8	19.8.66	MR Peter Buckley Raphns Broadbridge Heath Horsham Sx	NBP 160 D Rice Bros. 23 8 66
	EJS 9746	H	SN 6322/41			B 5/8											
	1E50275	7E51640-9	G66 2500			51639	Silver Blue/D. Blue	Henlys M/c 20.7.64 P J Leads	10.4.67	78543	TSC 2961 5031	885	895	7	20.7.66	Transferred from Henly M/c 10.3.67	
	EJS 8302	G	6322/41			B 15/7											
	1E50276	7E51593-9	G66-2475			51626	Sand/Lt. Tan	Henlys L. 3596	30.8.66	78831	TSC 3369	885	885	8	12.8.66	E G Hoddinott Esq The Mount Par Cornwall	HAF 446 Callington MTS Ltd 23-8-66
	EJS 9608		6322/41			B 15/7											
	1E50277	7E51639-9	G66-2528			51648	Cream/Black	Byatt 17782	8.9.66	75915		885	—	4	5.8.66	MR A Amison 19 Vicarage Cresent Caverswall Stoke on Trent Staffs	Second owner L Bakes Bycars Rd Cockshill Burslem Stoke on Trent JVT 434 Retail Stoke on Trent 7 9 66 ExPen
	EJS 8912	S	6322/41			B 5/8											
	1E50278	7E51577-9	C66-2526 - 43/14 PL			51645	Sherwood/Biscuit	Henlys L 3517 Ritchies	9.11.67	78191 36321	5040	885	885	8	30.8.66	Transferred London 17.3.67.	
	EJS 9620	HHSHHH	6322/41			B 5/8											
	1E50279	7E51608-9	C66-2527			51649	Cream/Black	Glovers 1419	30.1.67	75001	TSC 4445	885	885	12	2.8.66	—	
	EJS 9359	H	6322/41			B 5/8											
7.66	1E50280	7E51327-9	F66-186			51647	Primrose/Black	Henlys L. 3525	5.8.66	78199 CEH7289	TSC 3102	885	904	8	8.8.66	MR J.M.C. Harder, Thames House, Woodlands Rd, Leigh on Sea Essex	J.H.J. 378 H.L. Abbot Motor 10. 8.
	EJ 10653	FSSSFS	6322/41			B 5/8											

A STUDY IN SIMPLICITY

IAN CALLUM,
JAGUAR DIRECTOR
OF DESIGN,
TALKS TO
STEPHEN BAYLEY
ABOUT WHAT IT
IS THAT MAKES
THE E-TYPE AN
AUTOMOTIVE
MASTERPIECE

"This," Ian Callum says to me, waving a simple T-shaped tool, "is literally the key to the entire car." On early E-Types, close to where the driver's offside knee would be in right-hand-drive versions, the T-shaped tool was held in place by spring clips. You needed it to open the huge, fantastically sculpted bonnet, although that is much too humble a term to describe such an ambitious and indulgent exercise in expressive metal.

Little chrome flaps cover apertures in the trailing edges each side of the bonnet. I fondly imagine that they were not the expression of a designer's whim, but the work of a man in overalls, ankle deep in swarf, on the shopfloor in Browns Lane. Anyway, lift the flaps, insert the tool and twist to release the sculpture. What follows is a theatrical revelation, an authentic psychological drama with mechanical actors. So much of erotic behaviour is characterised by postures of concealment and display: that is the act you participate in when you release the E-Type's bonnet. You are participating in theatre.

This is not mere inspection of an engine, it's the display of a machine's living heart; it's literally performance art. And this engine was so very clearly designed to be admired – those three SU carburettors lined-up by the polished cam boxes and the very self-conscious triangular air filter. Something of the childhood thrill of having a model car with opening doors applies to the full-size E-Type.

Closed, the bonnet is lascivious and gorgeous and the whole car seems poised for flight. Open, you enjoy a beautiful sort of intimacy. Suddenly, with the engine displayed, this fast car seems almost hobbled and is deliciously vulnerable and temptingly exposed. At some level, the people responsible understood very well the psychological dynamics of visual and tactile pleasure.

"So is it about erotic symbolism?" I ask Callum. "No," he replies emphatically. "I fell in love with the E-Type when I was seven or eight and you don't think about sex at that age." And then I say, "But people always describe its effect as phallic." "Not true," Callum replies, "The E-Type is much too voluptuous to be phallic." Of course, Callum's use of the word "love" is significant in this context. Sex, affection and beauty are naturally linked. And a lot of people think the E-Type Jaguar is the most beautiful car ever made. I mention this and Callum frowns a little then after a moment nods really quite keenly. "Certainly one of them" he says.

THERE IS A LOT OF
EXPRESSION
IN THIS CAR.
BUT ALSO A LOT
OF PURITY

We are at Whitley, Jaguar's design and technology facility in Coventry. It's a huge, deliberately featureless room so nothing distracts the management from concepts presented here for critical scrutiny. But we are looking not at next year's models, but at a 50-year-old car: the fourth E-Type ever built, in dark blue metallic with red leather; here to be aesthetically analysed by the two of us. And, we both agree, this interrogation will have the thoroughness of a courtroom cross-examination.

They used to say in a lazy old trope that in some portraits "the eyes follow you around the room". It's the other way around here, even after we have been in the room for two hours with no distractions, we cannot take our eyes off the E-Type. It sucks visual attention from its environment. How exactly has that been achieved?

"There's a lot of expression in this car," Callum explains. "But there is also a lot of purity." Malcolm Sayer was Jaguar's aerodynamicist who operated under the stern mathematical rules of his discipline. In the pre-silicon chip 1960s, Sayer's calculations were put to the test in a primitive wind tunnel that drew enough power to black out the nearby village. So the design team would retire to the local hostelry, hoist a few ales and wait until they saw the villagers retire for the night. When all the lights in the neighbouring houses were doused, the team knew they could seek the answers blowing in the wind. His slide rule calculations were found to be at most eight percent out.

Within these rules there was, however, quite a lot of scope for willful styling; Sayer admired the 1952 Alfa Romeo Disco Volante by Carrozzeria Touring of Milan, an astonishing composition of segments and sections of circles, which undoubtedly influenced the E-Type. But Sayer was also a musician. Miles Davis' *Kind of Blue* was released while the E-Type was in development. Davis' rule was "I don't play what's there, I play what's not there". Has there ever been a better description of the creative process? I wonder if Sayer listened to Davis.

As soon as you start analysing the E-Type with a tutored eye, all manner of strange aesthetic truths are revealed. Look at it in plan form and this 'voluptuous' car is actually a strict flat rectangle. Stand back at front three-quarters and you can soon see that the famous front wings are, in fact, nearly pure cylinders, just like a cigar tube. Yet it does not look as if it was designed with a compass and set square; our eyes are tricked into seeing the profile as a gorgeous designer's expressive 'flowline' because of that clever bit of metal-pressing on the door. A simple angled detail below the bottom of the side-glass creates an apparent continuity that gives the E-Type its distinctive presence.

The aesthetic is a genius amalgam of mathematics with bravura flourishes. To Ian Callum it is clear that Malcolm Sayer used geometry as a creative tool in the way designers today might use mood boards with pages torn from yachting and aerospace magazines as inspiration.

"What we see comes from the geometry needing to express itself. It is not free expression," he says. "Look at that," and he points to the trailing edge of the bonnet. "I bet that's a pure radius with an explicit mathematical value." That very well may be, but what makes this automobile composition so effective is that to the numerical facts of geometry are added the intangibles of art.

The proportions, for example, are expressionist. But look closely and you see that it is not so much a very long bonnet as a very short cabin; the E-Type is a rather small car, but its sensational appearance gives an impression of stature beyond its mere dimensions.

Then there is the power bulge. Of course, this helps articulate the aggression of a powerful sports car, but is also an absolutely inspired sculptural device. The inflamed power bulge adds a fascinating complexity and counterpoise to the geometry of the bonnet.

Other details? Callum says, "When I was a kid I used to draw the headlamp lens. It absolutely fascinated me. I realise now it was because its proportions are nearly 2:3, very close to The Golden Section of the ancients." Then there are brilliant details like the chrome bar that splits the air-intake, quite unnecessary, but distinctly characterful. I suspect we are back to the man ankle deep in swarf. The quarter bumpers have nothing at all to do with aerodynamics and everything to do with a stylist's sense of gorgeousness. The wrap-around rear bumpers are, "Beautiful, just beautiful. It's all about putting just enough style into a car to make it fascinating." Those masterful, horizontal rear lights? In fact they are standard units used vertically on the Mark X. Then there are the exhausts; like the power bulge, these were deliberately emphasised to create visual drama. Callum looks at the JAGUAR badge on the side-opening hatchback. This comprises simple engineer's letter-forms connected by a lower bar. "Lovely, utterly lovely," is Callum's verdict.

To my eye, the windscreen is strangely vertical, but Callum tells me this is a cause and effect of dramatic proportions. Interestingly, the resulting screen required a signature three wipers. To Callum's eye, the rear side window could have been lowered by an inch resulting in a changed expressive graphic of much greater dynamism. The track is unhelpfully narrow, with the wheels rather reticent in the bodywork but there is "so much form in the car" we do not really notice, so Sayer got away with it. There are practical faults, too; charmingly, the screws holding the headlamp trim in place have, apparently, been located at random and one of them appears on this car to be cross-threaded.

A different language is apparent in the cabin; it is very honest and very simple. The only wood is the steering wheel. What art there is can be found in the uncompromising manner of detail presentation; those four minor gauges in a martial row have become a recurrent Jaguar motif. The array of flick switches is a nice reminder that the E-Type was closer to the lash-up era of the Spitfire than it is to us. Of course, there is no sat-nav. Instead, you can flick a switch for the 'Map Light'. Those were simpler days.

Neither Callum nor I are especially tall, but the E-Type cabin cramps us both. You can forget about heel 'n' toe and even with the seat at the back of its runners, you sit over the wheel like a hungry gorilla embracing the trunk of a banana tree. "It was only Italians who wanted straight-arm driving positions," Callum says, "because it looked better." The cruel truth? It must have been very hard work to drive an E-Type. Those Sixties King's Road E-types – Terence Conran, Ringo Starr and Simon Dee – must have been addled with sweat and cramp before they lost sight of Sloane Square.

"Cars cause angst," Callum concludes, "but this is because they have so much emotional significance." I wondered, at last, if the Jaguar E-Type really deserves its place in New York's Museum of Modern Art, up against the sculpture of Brancusi and David Smith. "Yes. Absolutely justified," he says. "You could own an E-Type, never drive it and still love it."

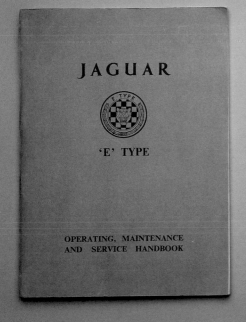

• • • •

ALWAYS READ THE MANUAL

The books that meant you were part of a select club - the original owners' manuals covering three (and a half...) generations of E-Type

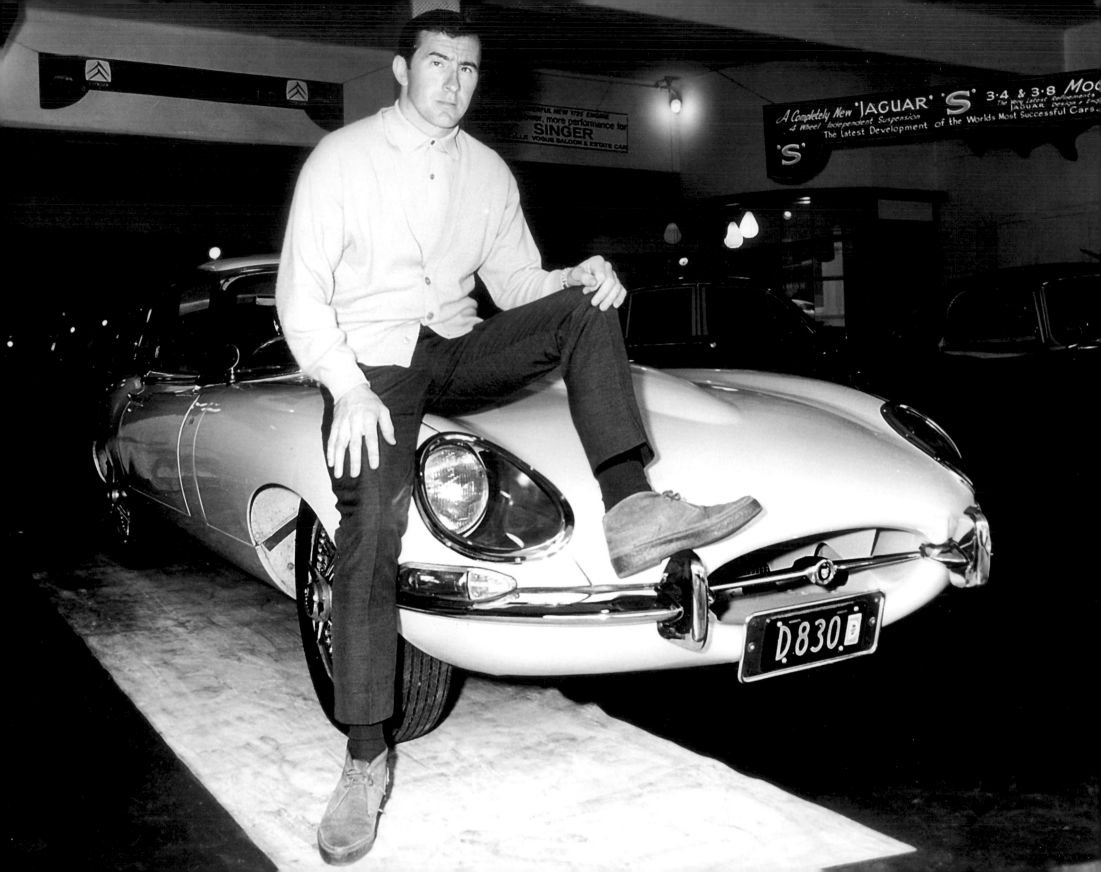

WHAT THE E MEANS TO ME

SIR JACKIE STEWART

The E-Type was not simply an iconic car but it played a huge part in my personal and professional life in the 1960s. My family actually ran a Jaguar dealership in Dumbarton and one of our best customers was a chap called Barry Filer, who allowed me to help him as a mechanic at races.

We were at a meeting at Oulton Park when I got the chance to drive an E-Type against some pretty big names of the era. I can remember everything about that car – even the number plate: FSN1. It was a garage demonstrator but I managed to set similar lap times to Roy Salvadori and that was probably the point at which I knew my future lay with motor racing rather than trap shooting, which was my other passion.

On the racetrack, the E-Type was immediately a winner in the hands of drivers like Graham Hill. It was very well balanced and had a very driveable engine, so it was relatively easy to drive quickly. It was a perfect car for someone starting out like me.

Away from the track it also helped me win over the future Mrs Stewart! Helen and I were walking out at that time, too, and we did a lot of miles in an E-Type together. It was the car in which she drove at 100mph for the first time – and I should add that there were no speed limits in those days... We also went on our honeymoon in one; we drove all the way to Germany, where I also competed in a shooting competition. I finished second... and I still blame Helen for that!

The E-Type's timeless design and speed made it one of the great cars in the history of the British motor industry. It's famous for being the car that everyone wanted and, at just a couple of thousand pounds, it was half the price of many of the limited edition cars from Ferrari, Aston and the like.

But it also played a part in changing how car owners dealt with dealers and the industry. It marked the beginning of the end for the specialist body builders because a network of dealerships was now in place, so you could easily fix your car if you bent it. That hadn't been the case before.

The E-Type was, in every sense, the first mass-produced sportscar in Britain. Nothing before had been available to so many people, for which we have Sir Williams Lyons to thank. He did so much for the motor industry in this country and it's hard to believe that he was never made a peer.

Nothing let this car down, particularly when it first came out. In its purest form, before it grew bigger bumpers and a higher roofline, it was an incredibly beautiful car. Its lines were so clean. It revolutionised motoring and everyone wanted one. Why have a Ferrari when you could have one of these?

● ● ● ●

A young Jackie Stewart poses with an E-Type – the car which brought him to motor racing... and helped him to win over his future wife

THE E-TYPE IN NUMBERS

HOW FAST,
HOW MUCH,
HOW MANY...
IT'S ALL HERE IN
THIS NUMERICAL
COMPENDIUM

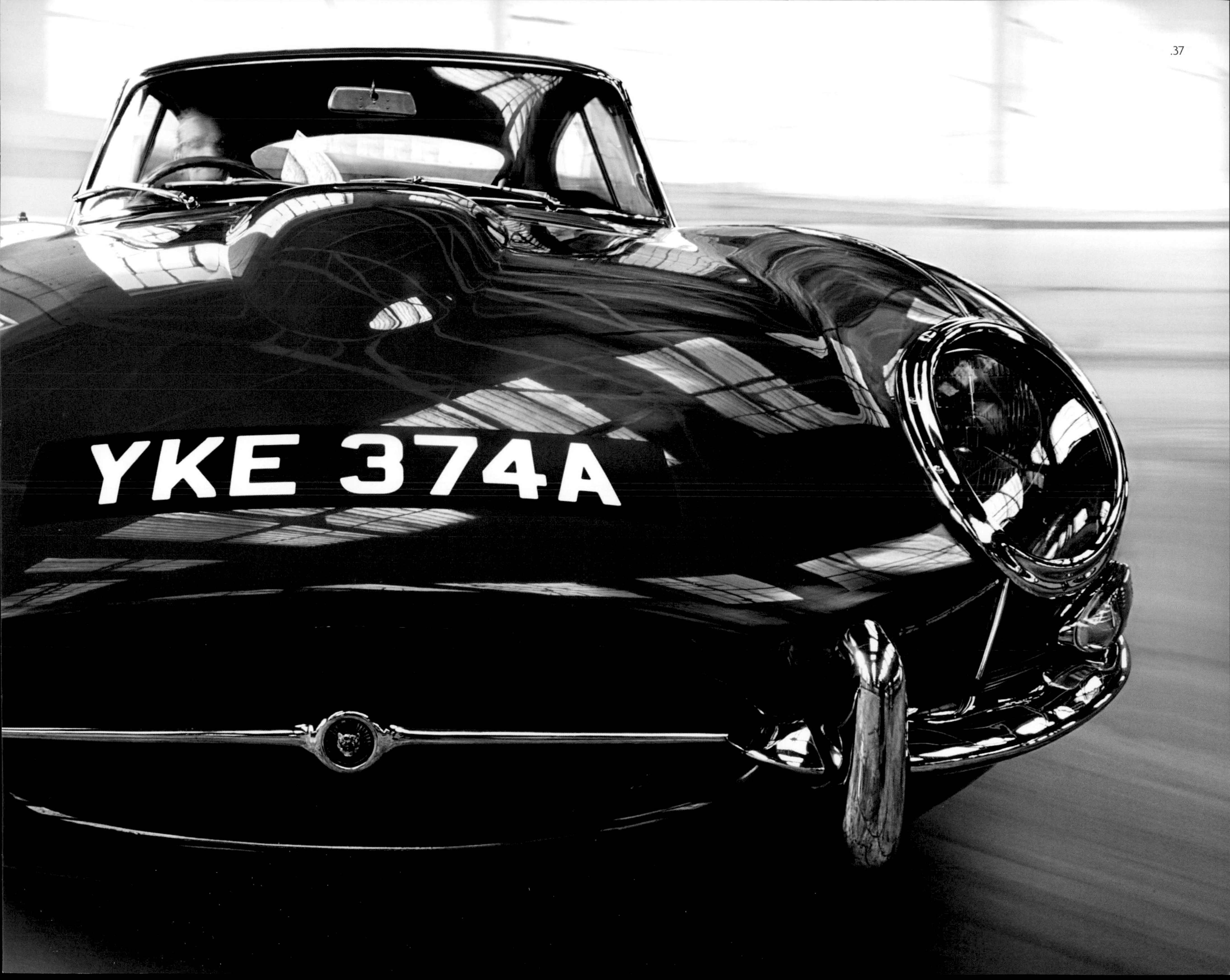
YKE 374A

There is no doubt that the E-Type possesses an elemental elegance, a shape that appears to have been formed by organic processes. It is an indication of Malcolm Sayer's genius that such sculpture could come from the principles of form following function. The aerodynamicist painstakingly designed the E-Type using slide rules and mathematical tables to plot its complex curves. Clearly numbers have played their part in the car's construction, as this collection of the E-Type's vital statistics shows.

THE E-TYPE WAS
PRESENTED TO THE
WORLD'S PRESS AT
THE RESTAURANT DU
PARC DES EAUX VIVES
IN GENEVA AT

4.30PM ON THE 15TH OF MARCH 1961

EXACTLY 1 MONTH LATER THE
E-TYPE WON ITS FIRST RACE OVER

25 TWISTY LAPS
OF THE OULTON PARK CIRCUIT,
DRIVEN BY FUTURE F1 WORLD
CHAMPION GRAHAM HILL

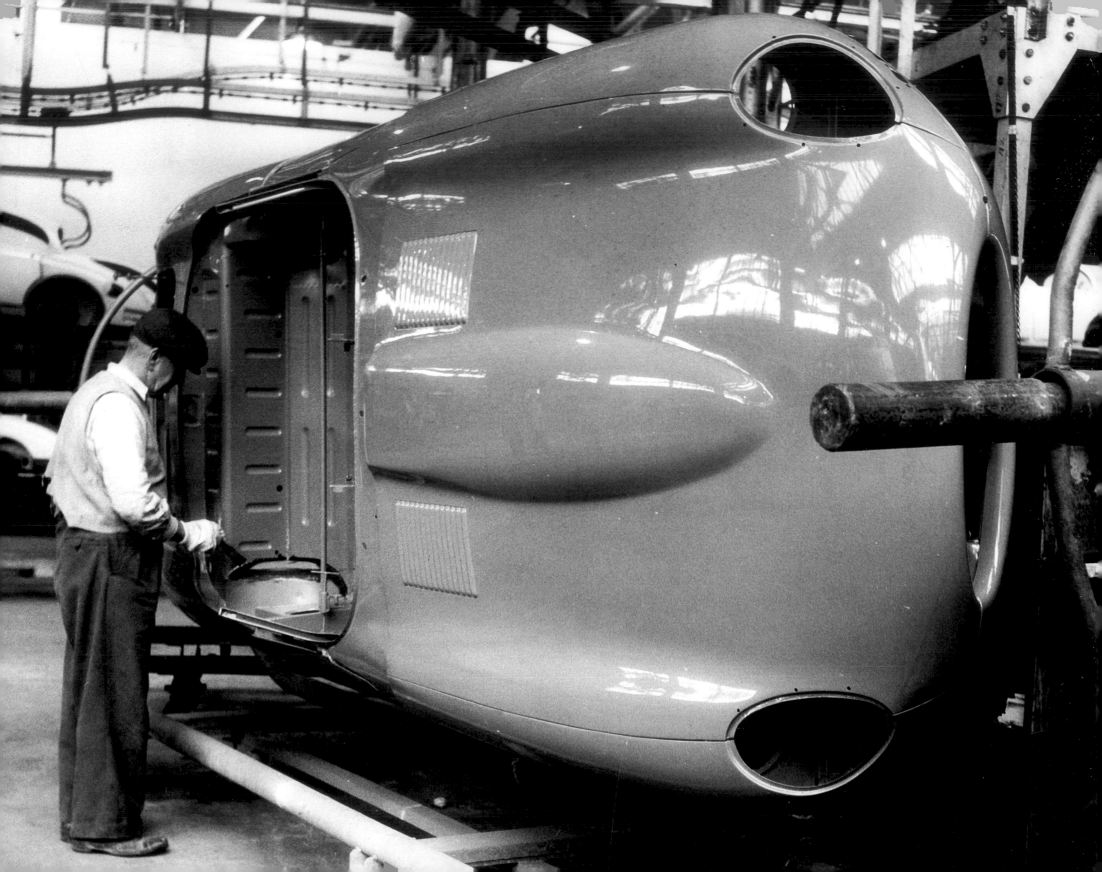

THE E–TYPE'S
RACING PEDIGREE
WAS REINFORCED,
IN 1962 WITH

4TH AND 5TH

PLACE FINISHES
AT LE MANS

THE E–TYPE'S
STRAIGHT–SIX
ENGINE HAD
POWERED JAGUAR
TO FIVE LE MANS
VICTORIES IN THE
1950S AND BY
1961 PRODUCED

265BHP AND 256LB FT

OF TORQUE

AN E-TYPE ROADSTER WEIGHED JUST 1206KG, ONLY 20 PERCENT MORE THAN THE ALUMINIUM-BODIED D-TYPE RACE CAR THAT PRECEDED IT

THE E-TYPE WAS A GENUINE 150MPH PROPOSITION AND, LIKE ITS XK120 PREDECESSOR,
THE FASTEST PRODUCTION CAR IN THE WORLD

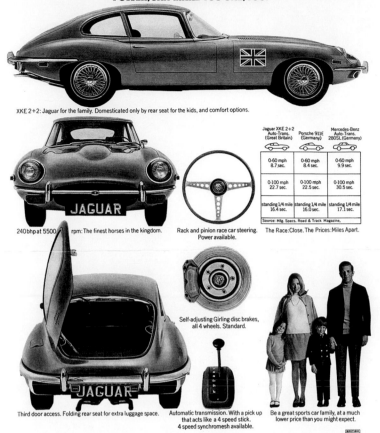

JAGUAR: THE CAR THAT MAKES GREAT BRITAIN A GREAT SPORTS CAR POWER, CAN MAKE YOU ONE, TOO.

XKE 2+2: Jaguar for the family. Domesticated only by rear seat for the kids, and comfort options.

	Jaguar XKE 2+2 Auto-Trans. (Great Britain)	Porsche 911E (Germany)	Mercedes-Benz 280SL (Germany) Auto-Trans.
0-60 mph	8.7 sec.	8.4 sec.	9.9 sec.
0-100 mph	22.7 sec.	22.5 sec.	30.5 sec.
standing 1/4 mile	16.4 sec.	16.0 sec.	17.1 sec.

Source: Mfg. Specs. Road & Track Magazine.

240 bhp at 5500 rpm: The finest horses in the kingdom.

Rack and pinion race car steering. Power available.

The Race:Close. The Prices:Miles Apart.

Self-adjusting Girling disc brakes, all 4 wheels. Standard.

Third door access. Folding rear seat for extra luggage space.

Automatic transmission. With a pick up that acts like a 4 speed stick. 4 speed synchromesh available.

Be a great sports car family, at a much lower price than you might expect.

For overseas delivery information write: Jaguar Cars 600 Willow Tree Road Leonia, New Jersey 07605

AT LAUNCH, THE E–TYPE COST £2,256, INCLUDING TAX AND THE ALL–IMPORTANT OPTIONAL WIRE WHEELS, THE EQUIVALENT TODAY OF £38,000

THE E–TYPE ACTUALLY GOT CHEAPER. A 1973 SERIES 3 WAS LISTED AT £3,378.38. IN TODAY'S MONEY THAT'S JUST £30,000

THE E–TYPE REMAINED IN PRODUCTION FOR **14 YEARS**. IT SOLD MORE THAN **72,000** UNITS, MAKING IT EUROPE'S FIRST MASS–PRODUCED SPORTS CAR BUT ONLY **12,000** WERE EARMARKED FOR BRITAIN

WHAT
THE

MEANS
TO
ME

JAY LENO

I've always loved cars but growing up in small town New England, I just didn't see any exciting ones. It was a working-class kind of place, everyone had traditional four-door American sedans.

Then one day I was out on my bike and this guy was rolling his XK120 out of the garage. I just stopped and stared, I was stunned, mesmerised. I thought it was the most exciting car I had ever seen and then when the XKE came along, as impossible as it seemed, it topped it. I just thought: "Oh my God, how can they keep doing this?"

It looked like the future and more than that, because it was a Jaguar, it seemed attainable. The XKE was a car that a working-class person, if they applied themselves, played their cards right and were reasonably successful, could own one day.

The XKE was the beautiful girl next door, the prettiest girl in your neighbourhood who, when you looked at her, you realised was better looking than any unattainable supermodel.

It was a car you could work on yourself as well and being able to do minor repairs and servicing is what really bonds you with a car. When I was a kid there was a saying about taking a car out for an 'XKE tune-up' which basically meant taking it out on the highway and flooring it and they sure seemed to run better after that!

As a piece of artwork it is stunning; it looks like it is moving when it's parked by the sidewalk. And the thing is, people gravitate towards it. Park it anywhere and when you get back, there will be a pretty girl sitting in it. It was the first car I remember girls responding positively to, it appealed to both sexes equally. Penelope Cruz came over to my garage one day and she went right over to the Jag and said: "Oh my God, that's the most beautiful car in the world."

I've owned my XKE for 18 years now and it's still wonderful to drive – the classic British sports car experience. It was so far ahead of its time that it doesn't take much to bring an XKE up to modern standards. Mine takes things a bit further though. It has the beautiful Series 1 body on a chopped Series 3 chassis with that wonderful V12. Drive other exotics and people think you're a poseur but I don't know anyone who doesn't love the XKE. Even in Hollywood everyone gives you the thumbs up...

There are only a few industrial designs that are perfect: the Coke bottle, the Kodak camera and the XKE. It is impossible to improve on the way it looked when it left the factory; it's the most iconic sports car of the 20th century.

● ● ● ●

Chat show host – and self-confessed car nut – Jay Leno poses
with his XKE roadster, which has a Series 1 body beneath which
hide the chassis and V12 engine from the later Series 3 model

ALL THINGS FOR ALL PEOPLE, EVERYWHERE... A motto like that made Harrods the ideal place to show off the new Series 3 to the public.

IN MACRO

IT'S TIME TO TAKE
A CLOSER LOOK AT
A DESIGN CLASSIC
FROM ANGLES
YOU MIGHT
NEVER HAVE
SEEN BEFORE...

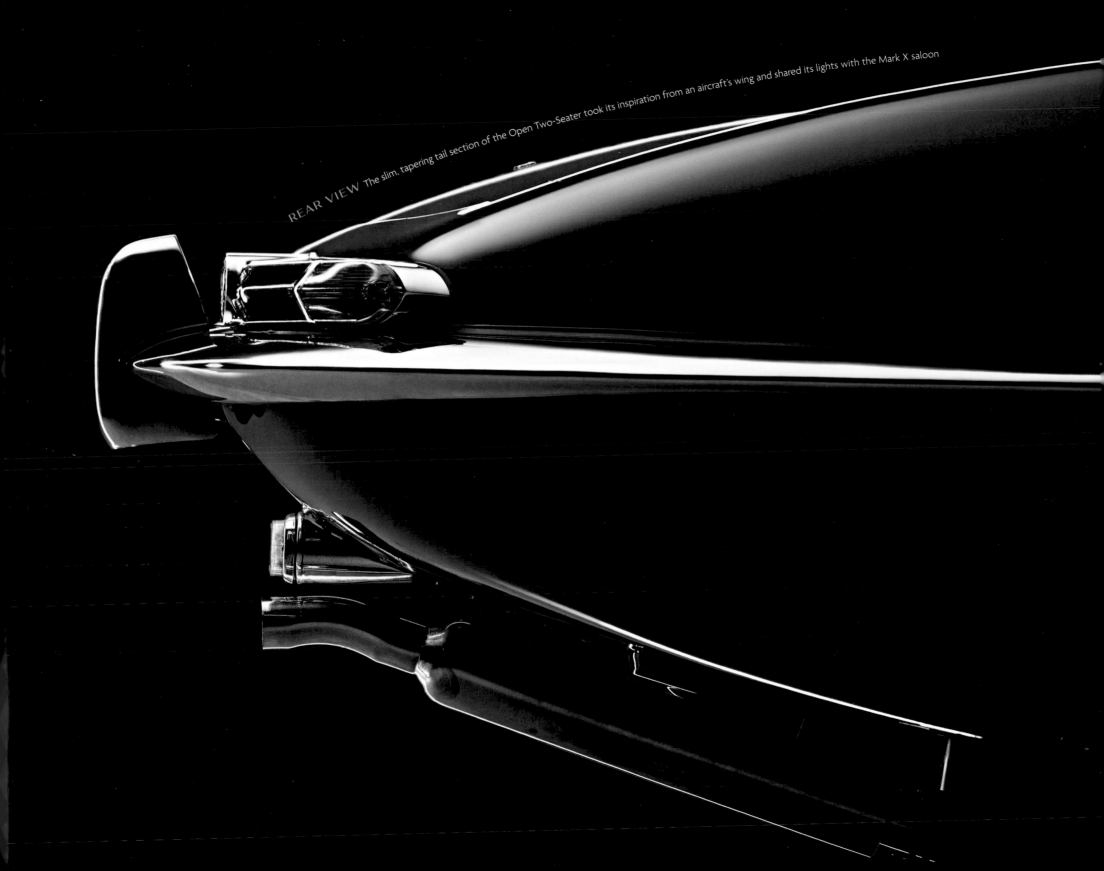

REAR VIEW The slim, tapering tail section of the Open Two-Seater took its inspiration from an aircraft's wing and shared its lights with the Mark X saloon

LIGHT FANTASTIC

The covered headlights took their cue from earlier Le Mans-winning Jaguars and helped the E-Type achieve its record-breaking 150mph top speed but didn't do much for night-time visibility

SPINNING WHEEL

They completed the design beautifully but, surprisingly, the all-important wire wheels with their racing car-type centre spinners were a cost option

DASHING GOOD LOOKS The dashboard of the Series 1 was beautifully finished in machine-turned aluminium set off by the simple Smiths instruments and straightforward toggle switches

INTERIOR | BRIGHT DIM PANEL | FAST SLOW FAN | IGNITION

SMITHS

OIL

LB/□"

20 40 60

SMITHS

WATER

°C

70 110

AR   STARTER   MAP   FAST
                                                    SLOW
                                                    WIPER   WASHER

A CERTAIN RATIO Hard to believe that the E-Type achieved such astonishing performance with what would nowadays be regarded as less than the full complement of gears

CARB LOADING

The E-Type's engine was almost identical to that of the last of the racing D-Types. It exchanged Weber carburettors for SU units; trading a little top-end power for low-down torque to aid real-world road manners

VIEW FROM THE TOP

The transmission tunnel is one of the few straight lines you will find on an E-Type.
Beautifully trimmed, the interior of the car reflected the stripped-down purity of the exterior.
But Jaguar did throw in an extra windscreen wiper for free...

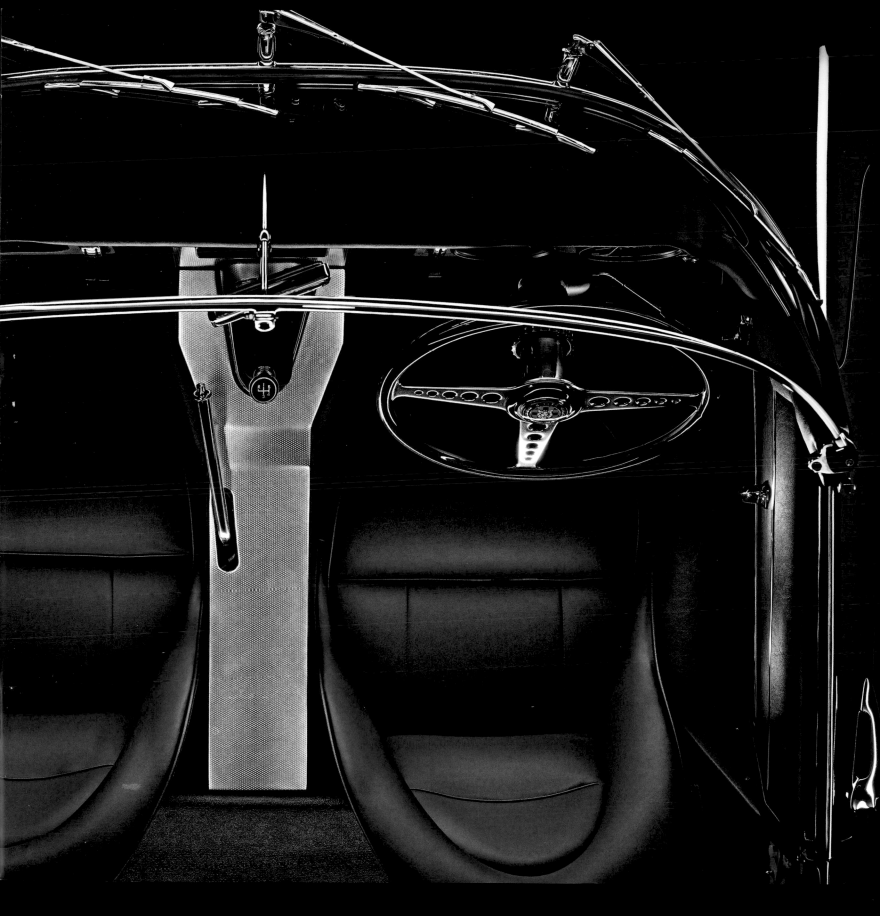

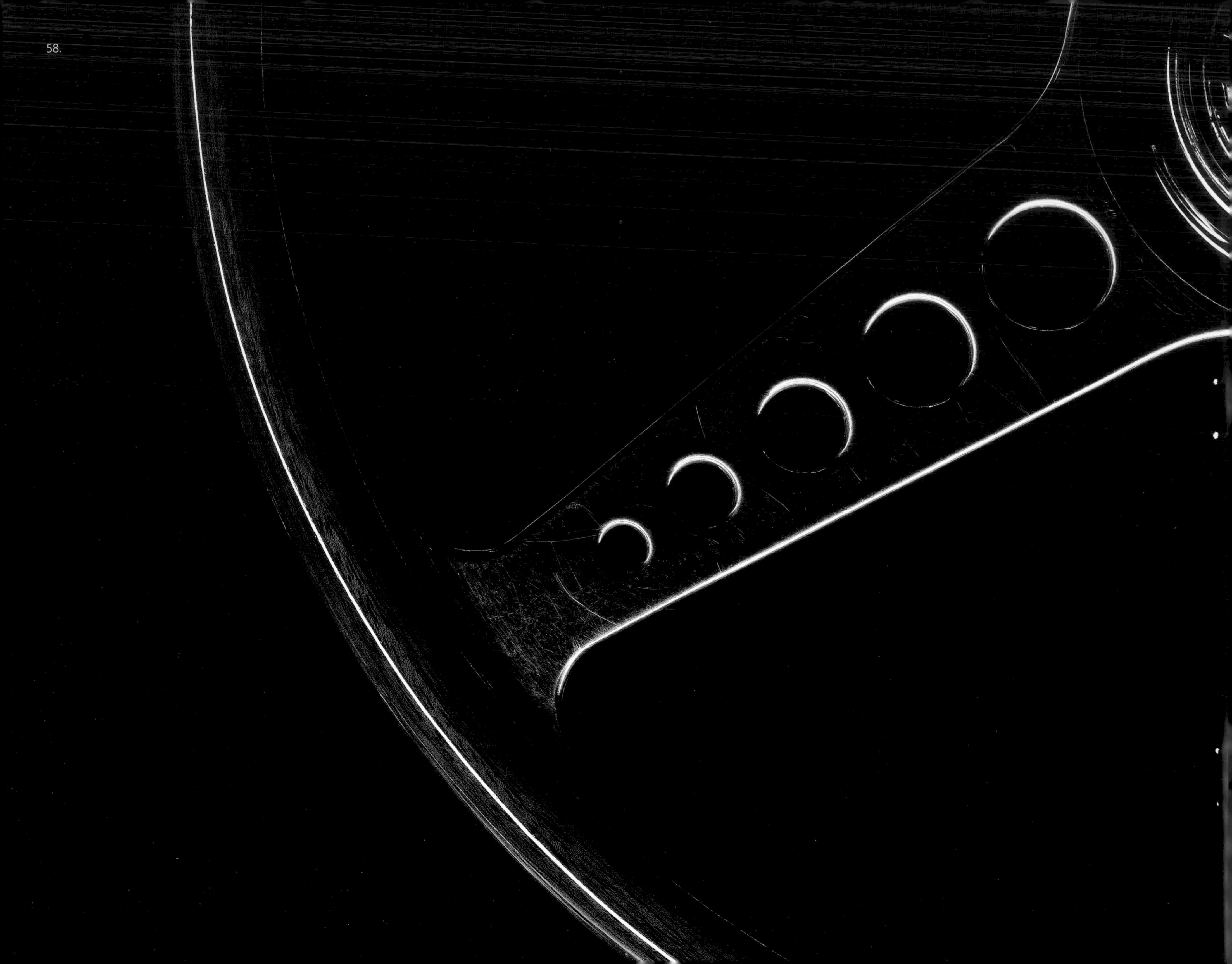

The only part of the E-Type that could be called traditional was the three-spoke metal and wood steering wheel whose thin rim proved a tactile delight

BEHIND THE WHEEL

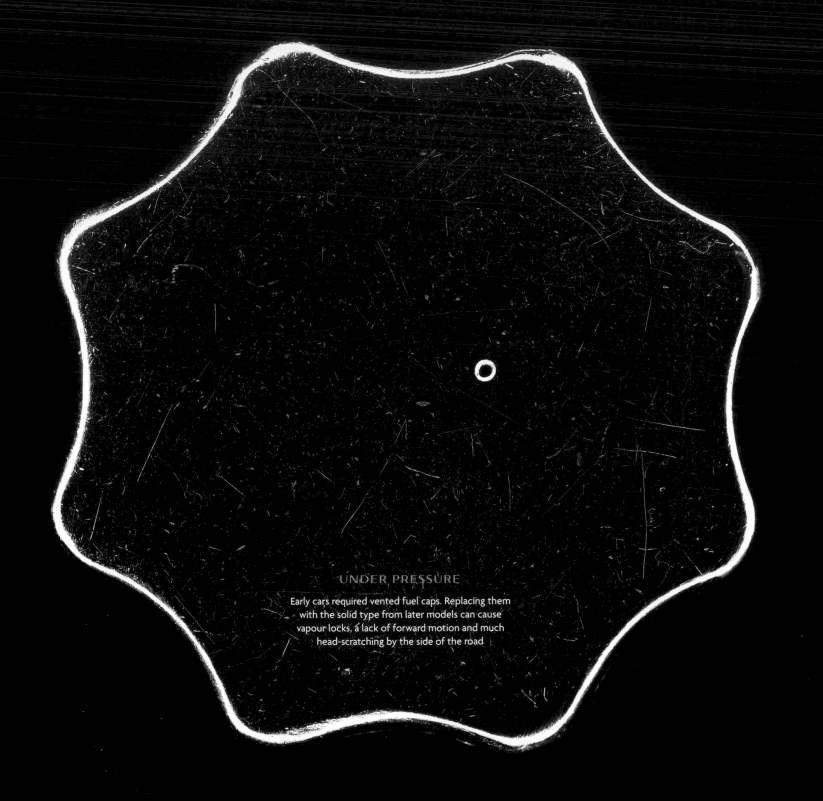

UNDER PRESSURE

Early cars required vented fuel caps. Replacing them
with the solid type from later models can cause
vapour locks, a lack of forward motion and much
head-scratching by the side of the road

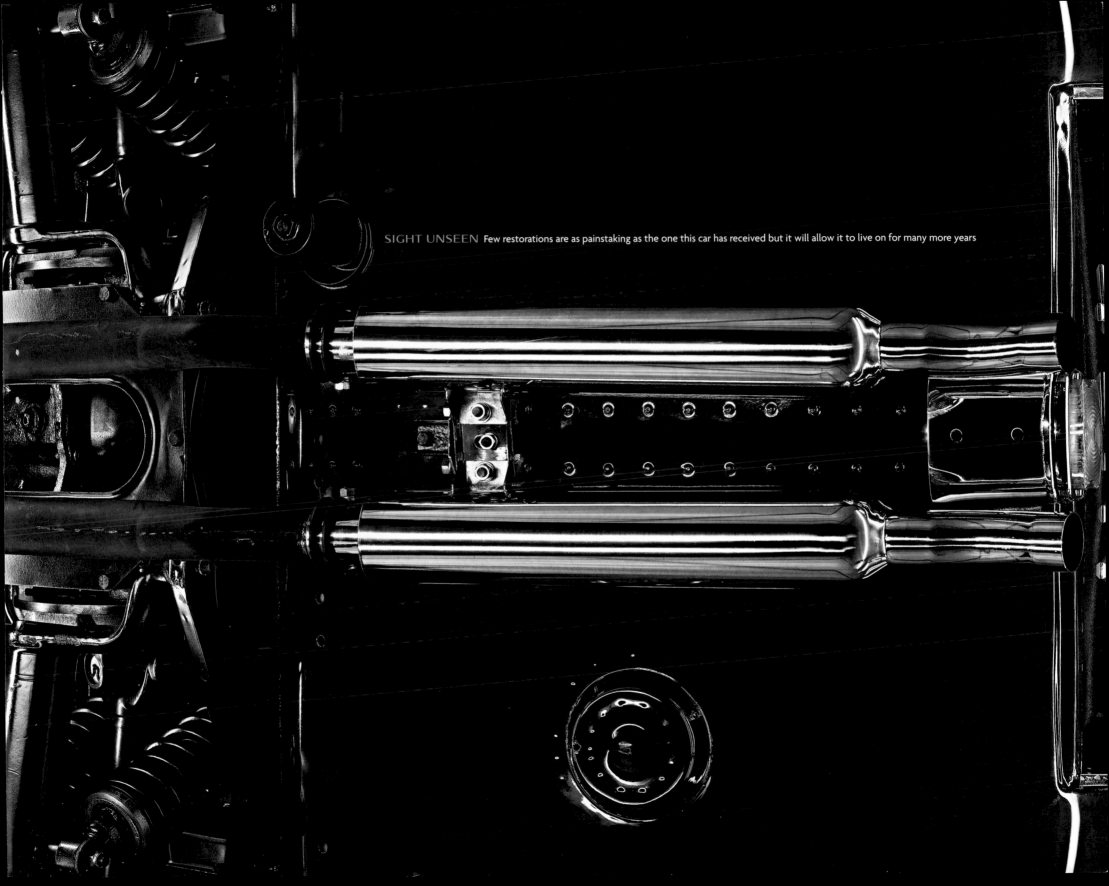

SIGHT UNSEEN Few restorations are as painstaking as the one this car has received but it will allow it to live on for many more years

WHAT
THE
MEANS
TO
ME

MARTIN BRUNDLE

I began racing for Jaguar nearly 30 years ago, starting with the Tom Walkinshaw XJ-S that won the European Touring Car Championship in 1984.

I was back a decade later as their lead driver and, in fact, all of my sports car racing victories – 18 out of 67 starts – were in Jaguars, everywhere from Le Mans to Daytona. That may be where my affection for Jaguar stems from but my memories of the E-Type are from a much younger age.

My father was a car dealer in Norfolk and, being a bit of a petrolhead, built up the area's leading sports car centre. My mum would drive me to school in an E-Type and I only had to open the back door of our house to see row upon row all lined up! As a kid I remember sitting behind the wheel and revving the engine and I suppose the first time I drove one would have been sitting in my father's lap and steering while he worked the pedals.

Officially though, the first one I drove in anger was CUT 7, the famous Dick Protheroe low-drag coupé, at one of the first Goodwood Revival meetings alongside Jack Brabham. The E-Type was fundamentally a great car to drive because there was so much carry-over from the C-Type and D-Type racers.

They handle well, put their power down nicely and do what you expect them to do, which is a fundamental requirement for a racing car.

I'd always hankered after one and after that I started keeping an eye out for a suitable car. Funnily enough, it was my helicopter that got me into an E-Type in the end, as I needed to keep my licence hours up and dropped in on a dealer on the South coast. I came home the proud owner of a red Series 3 convertible. It's been subtly upgraded with modern cooling, brakes and tyres, so it sits beautifully and handles so well. Very few cars of that era can still keep up with modern traffic but I can happily jump in it and cover 500 miles with no problem. Imagine the excitement it must have generated in 1961 by being able to hit 150mph. It was just so far ahead of its time it would have just blown people away.

It always looked sensational and I think it has got better with age. The great thing when driving it is the way people move over and let it past so they can have a look at it. I take it out whenever it feels right; you remember every journey in a car like that.

● ● ● ●

Formula 1 driver and Jaguar sports car legend Martin Brundle grew up surrounded by E-Types in his father's car dealership. Four decades later he became the proud owner of his very own Series 3 convertible

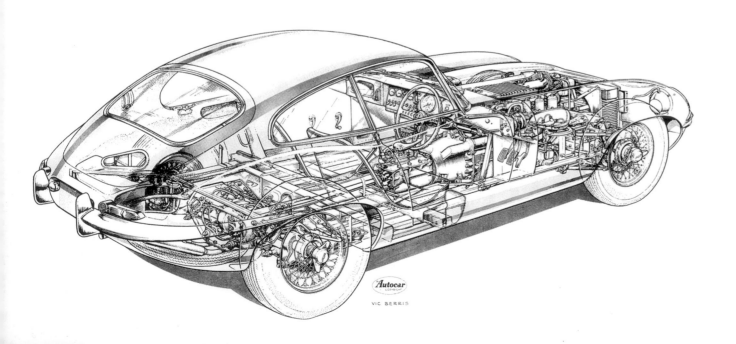

Autocar
VIC BERRIS

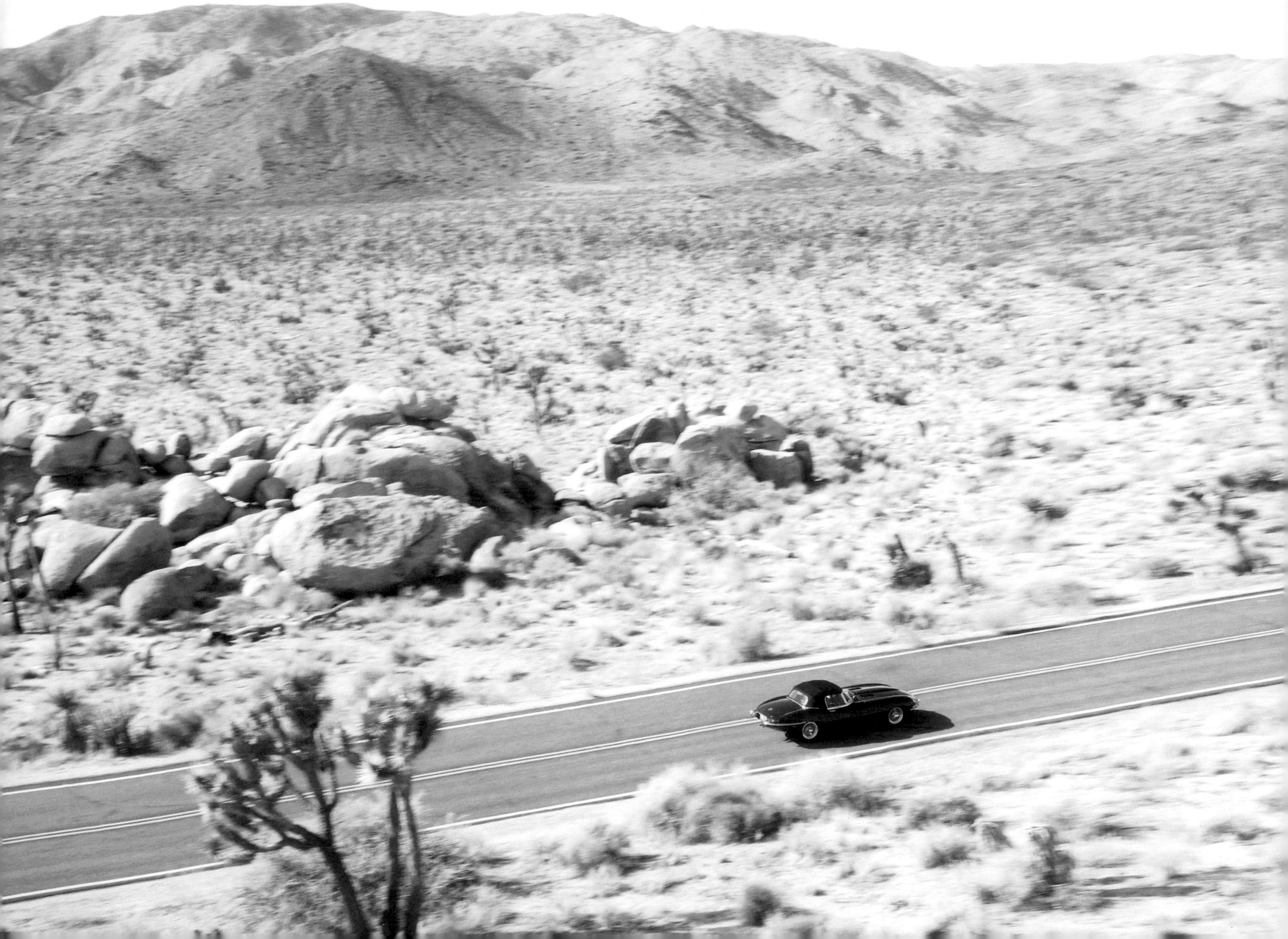

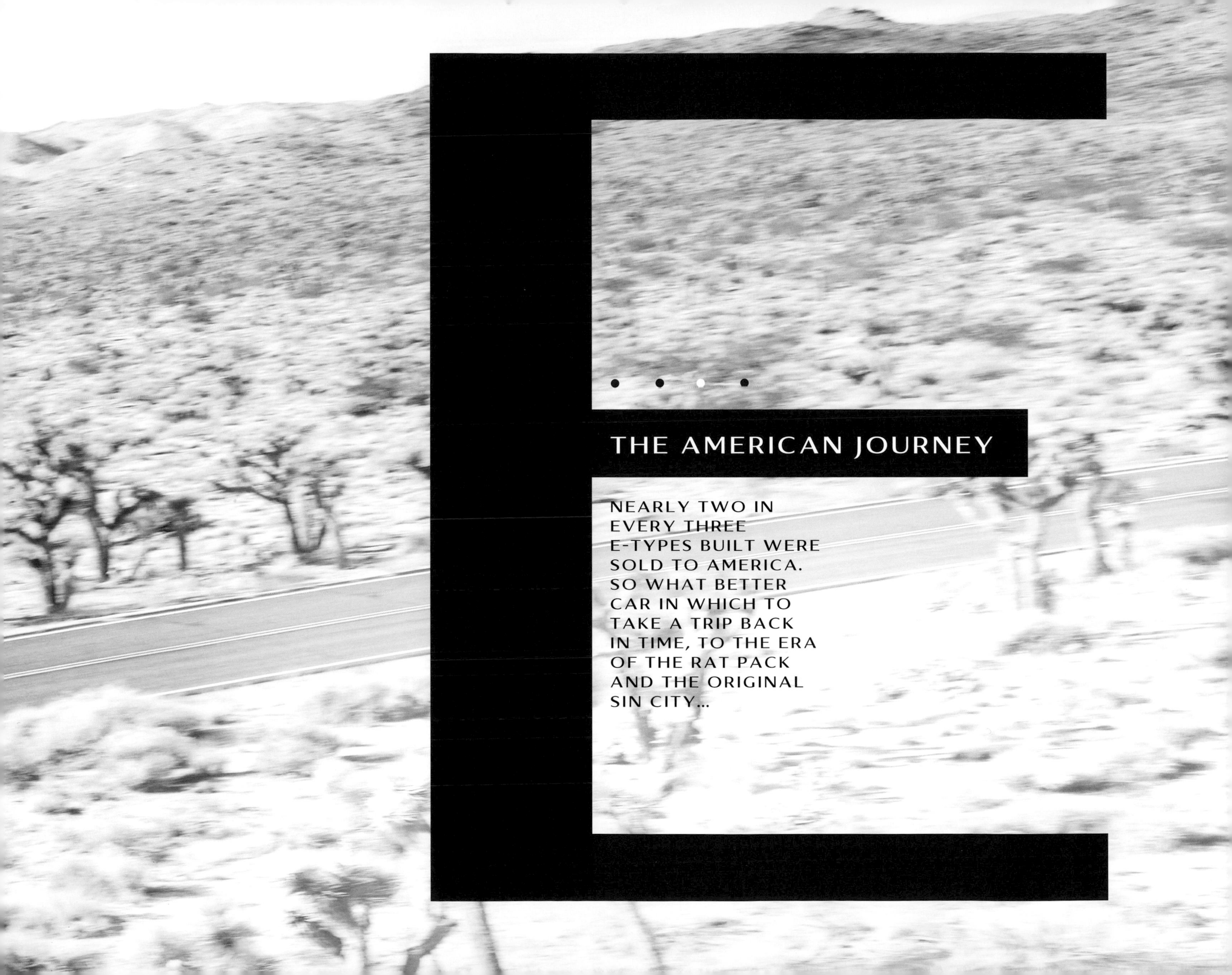

THE AMERICAN JOURNEY

NEARLY TWO IN
EVERY THREE
E-TYPES BUILT WERE
SOLD TO AMERICA.
SO WHAT BETTER
CAR IN WHICH TO
TAKE A TRIP BACK
IN TIME, TO THE ERA
OF THE RAT PACK
AND THE ORIGINAL
SIN CITY...

A

T 120MPH, with no cops or other traffic in sight, an E-Type is still impressive for a car that went on sale half a century ago. It tracks as straight and true as a Union Pacific locomotive, the steering wheel rock steady in your hands, the suspension settled and the body riding flat and true…

Long before the Eagles were extolling the virtues of a convertible and an empty desert highway, the E-Type was captivating West Coasters as surely as it had the Carnaby Street regulars. The E was a different kind of cool compared to the Californian hot-rods. One that required no customising; a more measured, altogether classier proposition that captured the louche appeal of the most envied and imitated men of the era – the Rat Pack.

And the hippest and hottest joints in all of America at the time were the Pack's stomping grounds – the casinos in Las Vegas, Nevada and the houses of Palm Springs, California, where they hung out when they weren't making movies in Hollywood.

The Jaguar E-Type (or XKE as it was known in the States) bowed in to sensational reviews at the 1961 New York Show, a month after it had wowed the press at the Geneva Auto Salon. The XK120 had first made Americans aware of Jaguar, but the E-Type took that interest to a new level, to the extent that around two-thirds of the 72,000 or so E-Types built between 1961 and 1974 were sold in the U.S.

The E-Type was big news from the outset, insinuating itself so far into popular culture that Jan and Dean sang about a race between a Corvette Sting Ray and an E-Type in the 1964 hit *Dead Man's Curve*. Chevrolet's glassfibre sports car was a natural competitor, the 350-horsepower convertible being a tad faster, at least in a straight line, and a touch cheaper at $5,275 compared with $5,525 for the E-Type in 1965.

Magazines like *Car and Driver* raved about the E-Type when they tested it. "There's something so sensual, so elemental in the appeal of the XKE that few men can resist its siren song," eulogised the magazine in a 1965 road test of a 4.2 convertible.

So it proves on the streets of Palm Springs, no stranger to a host of high-end automobiles, where the E-Type still looks massively cool. Palm Springs was established in 1853 by a government survey party, which noted the natural hot springs. The town rose to prominence during the days of the draconian Hollywood studio system, which demanded that stars be on standby no more than two hours away. Palm Springs, with its restful micro-climate became the retreat of choice and, allegedly, the scene of many an illicit assignation between leading men and ladies.

THERE'S SOMETHING
SO ELEMENTAL IN
THE APPEAL OF
AN E-TYPE THAT
FEW CAN RESIST
ITS SIREN SONG

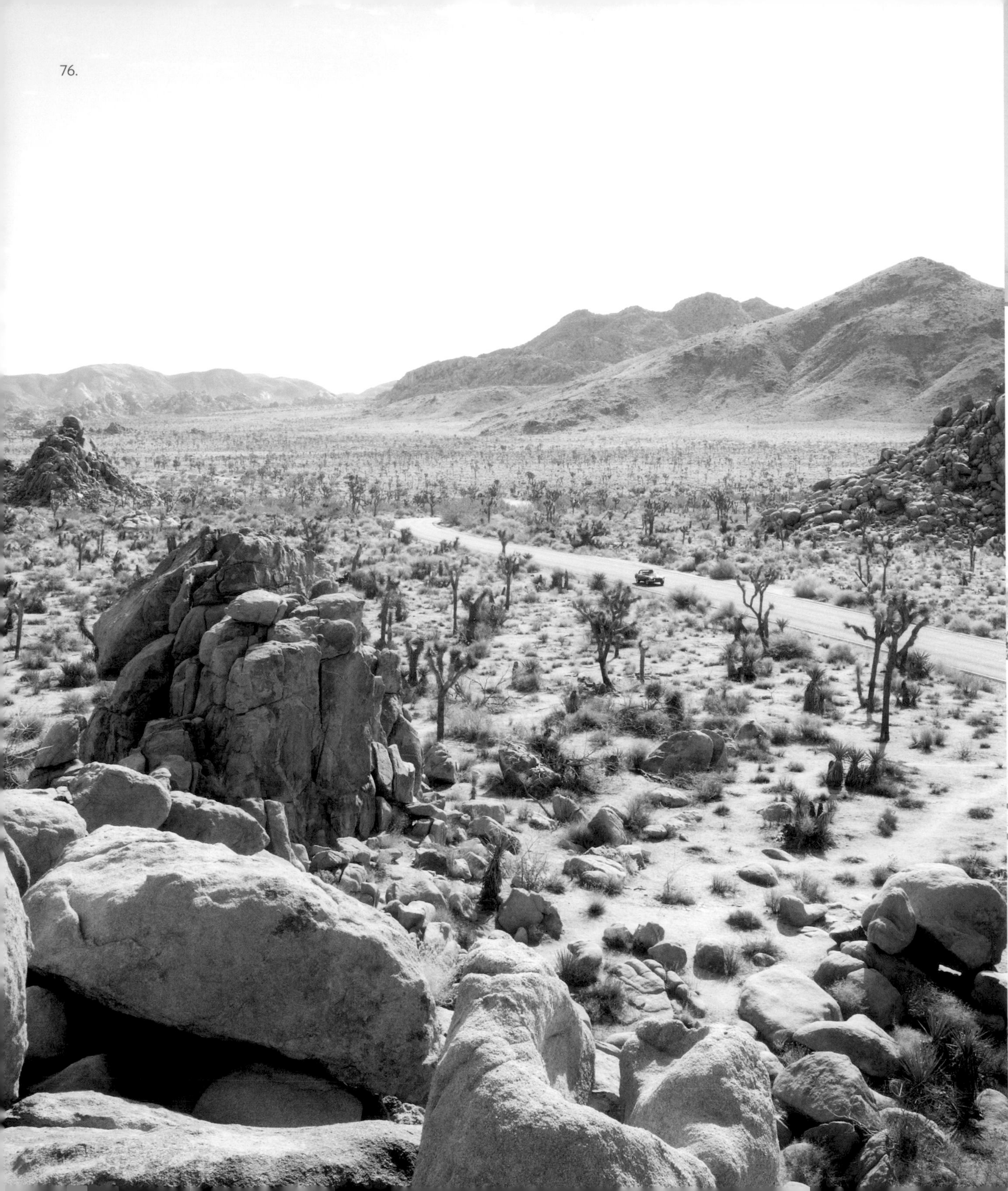

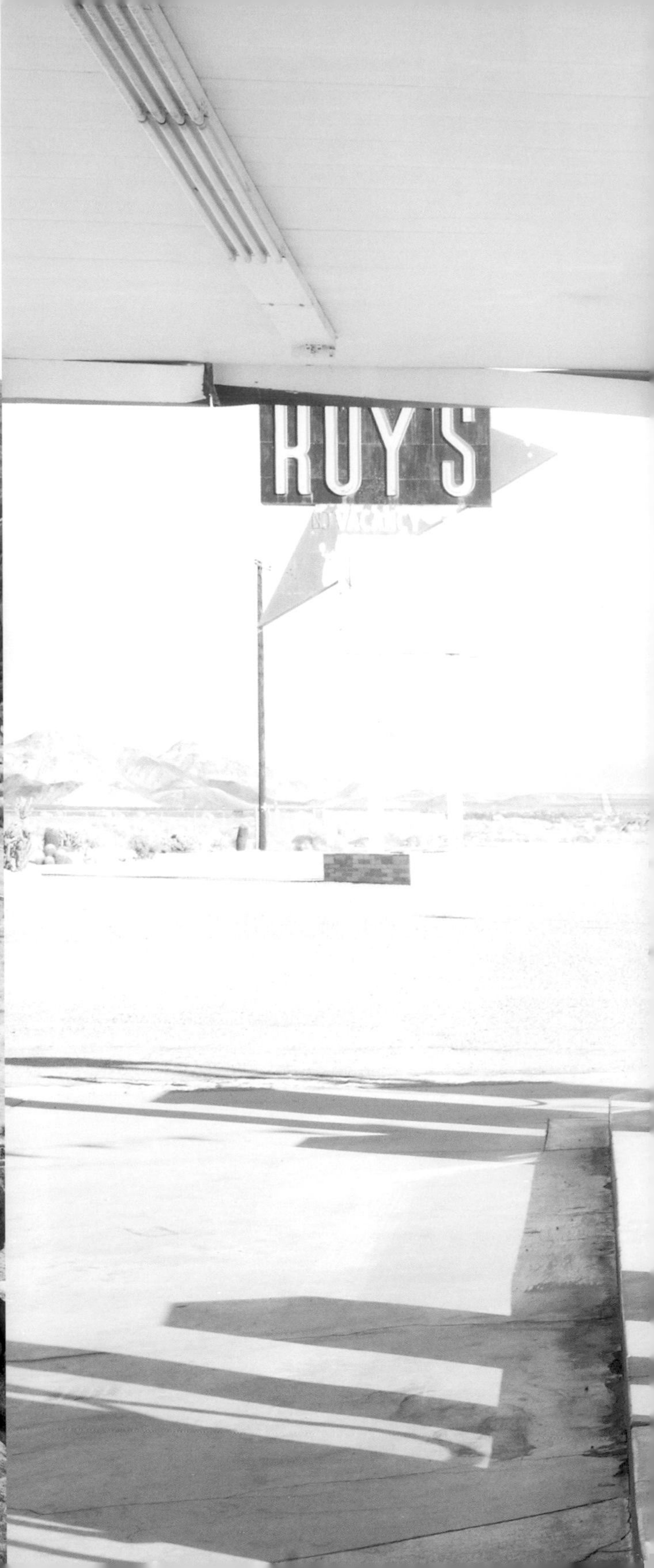

Frank Sinatra was one of the first Hollywood stars to build a home here, in an architectural style that became a Palm Springs signature: Desert Modernism. Twin Palms on Alejo Road is a relatively modest four-bedroom house with a piano-shaped pool, designed by E Stewart Williams in 1947. Elvis Presley and Priscilla spent their honeymoon in a home that had been labelled the House of Tomorrow and Dean Martin lived in an unassuming low-rise on Via Monte Vista. The landmark building in Palm Springs, though, is just up the street from Martin's; the fabulous glass, steel and stone Kaufmann House, designed by Richard Neutra and completed in 1946.

Like the E-Type, Palm Springs buildings such as the City Hall and Bank of America building have stood the test of time thanks to their inherent purity of form. The architectural lines may be straight rather than sensual but both share a sculptural beauty born of simplicity.

To see if the E-Type cuts the mustard today, we head north from Palm Springs towards Las Vegas. The car – a 1967 Series 1 4.2 roadster – is still a beauty, its compound curves highlighted by the crisp desert sunlight. An E-Type looks delicate and dainty on today's roads, especially alongside the monstrous sport-utility vehicles that dominate American highways. It feels petite from the cabin, too, with its close-set buckets, although it has reasonable legroom.

The E-Type's cabin is pure and simple compared with modern cars, its bank of white-on-black Smiths gauges evocative not only of the D-Type racer but also WW2 fighter planes like the Spitfire. The array of toggle switches, huge wood-rimmed steering wheel and the simple black trim are business-like and intuitive. The pedal-box is narrow and you sit high relative to the cowl and doors, but the bucket seats are comfortable. The car has an AM/FM radio, but we preferred to let the XK engine make the music on our drive to Vegas.

The sweeping curves and rolling terrain in the north-western part of the Joshua Tree National Park would be ideal E-Type territory, but the low speed limits mean we dial back and take in scenery that's dominated by the eponymous trees, the landscape lent an extra sense of grandeur by the San Jacinto Mountains looming in the background.

Once out of the park the road opens up, one of those arrow-straight pieces of tarmac that heads off to the horizon far beyond that curvaceous bonnet. Time to give the straight-six engine some stick. The E-Type isn't massively fast off the line, but the mid-range is superb, the torrent of torque from 2500rpm compelling. The all-synchromesh four-speed manual is much nicer than the clunky Moss 'box of earlier 3.8-litre E-Types, but it still has long throws and needs deliberate handling.

UNDER THE BRIGHT LIGHTS OF VEGAS, THE E-TYPE LOOKS AS GOOD AS IT DID IN THE HIGH DESERT

The engine makes a muted growl as the rev counter needle swings around to 5000rpm, its timbre tamed by a stainless-steel exhaust system.

The E-Type is one of those cars that bridges the ages, having the drivability and speed to still be used everyday plus the charm and immediacy of a vintage machine, especially the delicious mechanical connections between hands and steering and your foot and the throttle. We tend to think of E-Types as sports cars, but they were supercars in their time. Family saloons of the era such as a Morris 1300 would struggle to beat 80mph, yet an E-Type was a genuine 150mph car.

At Amboy, we turn onto Route 66, the artery that connected Los Angeles to Chicago until the Interstate freeway system was implemented, at which point towns such as this went from thriving waypoints to ghost settlements. Roy's Motel and Café dates back to 1938 and was expanded to include the mid-century motel in the 1950s, when the road was so busy that the owners of the gas station could charge travellers 10 cents a time to use the bathroom.

Our stint on Route 66 is short, as we swing left onto the Kelbaker Road, which cleaves the desert between mountains either side of the wide valley floor. Occasionally we encounter long, sweeping bends where the E-Type is poised, the steering accurate and faithful and grip from the 205-section tyres reasonable. The disc brakes are easy to modulate and powerful for a car from the 1960s, if a little anaemic by modern standards. The combination of supple ride and throttle-controllable handling is a template that Jaguar has done well to adhere to since the E-Type.

We arrive at Kelso in the Mojave National Preserve as the light fades and the sun dips close to the Providence Mountains. The town boomed as a WW2 staging post for troops but now all that remains is a wonderful 1924 Spanish Revival-style Union Pacific railroad station, restored and reinvented as a visitor centre.

It's cold now and I'm grateful that we've put the hood up because the heater was struggling to cope while driving *al fresco* towards Cima. When we cross the Nevada state line on I-15, a sea of neon greets us. The Rat Pack wouldn't recognise Sin City these days. The only names left on the Strip from their 50s and 60s heydays are the Riviera, Flamingo, Sahara and Tropicana, and only bits remain of the original hotels. In the Sahara, for instance, the entrance room to the House of Lords steakhouse survives. This is where the Pack each tipped a comely waitress $1000 in 1964, an astronomical sum when the average income in the U.S. at that time was $6600.

Vegas in the 1960s was split between Downtown — where casinos like the El Cortez and Golden Nugget operated — and the Strip, where the Sands and the Sahara were the glamorous alternatives. In those days, the hotels looked more like the low-rise motor inns that still populate Palm Springs, only bigger and glitzier. Then, as now, Vegas lured tourists with gambling and entertainers like the Rat Pack — who were an institution at the Sands — and Liberace, who was a staple at the Riviera. The Roman-themed Caesar's Palace was later a Sinatra favourite, a place he regularly played after falling out with the management at the Sands over unpaid gambling debts.

Today, Vegas runs the gamut from cheap, all-you-can-eat buffets to the fanciest, celebrity-chef restaurants you can imagine, from relatively chintzy hotels like Circus Circus to five-star hangouts like Wynns and Mandalay Bay. Unlike Palm Springs, which is low-key and classy, Vegas is the American dream on steroids, a place where a bar girl can hope she'll make it with a high roller like Tiger Woods or a factory worker can win big on the slots.

As we cruise around Vegas, we learn that the E-Type still strikes a chord with Americans. People sidle up to have their photo taken in front of the car or whip out their cell phones to take a picture of it. Even people who have no idea what an E-Type is, say "Cool car, Man." Under the bright neon lights that burn into the night sky, the E-Type looks as good as it did in the high desert and in the more genteel surroundings of Palm Springs. Even in this brashest of settings the E-Type remains a cut above.

In a city that is continuously looking for the next gimmick, the E-Type somehow manages not to appear just any old classic but exudes a timelessness and air of constancy. Like the Rat Pack, the E-Type proves that class never goes out of style.

LIKE THE RAT PACK, THE E-TYPE PROVES THAT CLASS NEVER GOES OUT OF STYLE

THE AMAZING ADVENTURES OF NORMAN DEWIS

DEWIS AND THE DASH TO GENEVA

Coventry

JAGUAR

THE E-TYPE DIDN'T JUST TAKE THE CROWDS

at the Geneva Motor Show by surprise, its rapturous reception caught Jaguar on the back foot as well.

Just one demonstrator, the fixed head 9600 HP, had been driven to Geneva by Jaguar press officer Bob Berry and after being presented to the media it was pressed into service showing off its abilities on a nearby hillclimb course.

Unsurprisingly, the queue was almost as long as the course itself and Berry soon found himself swamped. There was one other E-type available, 77 RW. The problem was that the convertible was being used as a development car, so it was nearly a thousand miles away, pounding round a British test track in the hands of Jaguar's chief test driver Norman Dewis.

A call was made and Dewis's session on the high-speed banking was interrupted by the track manager who told him he was wanted back at Browns Lane double-quick.

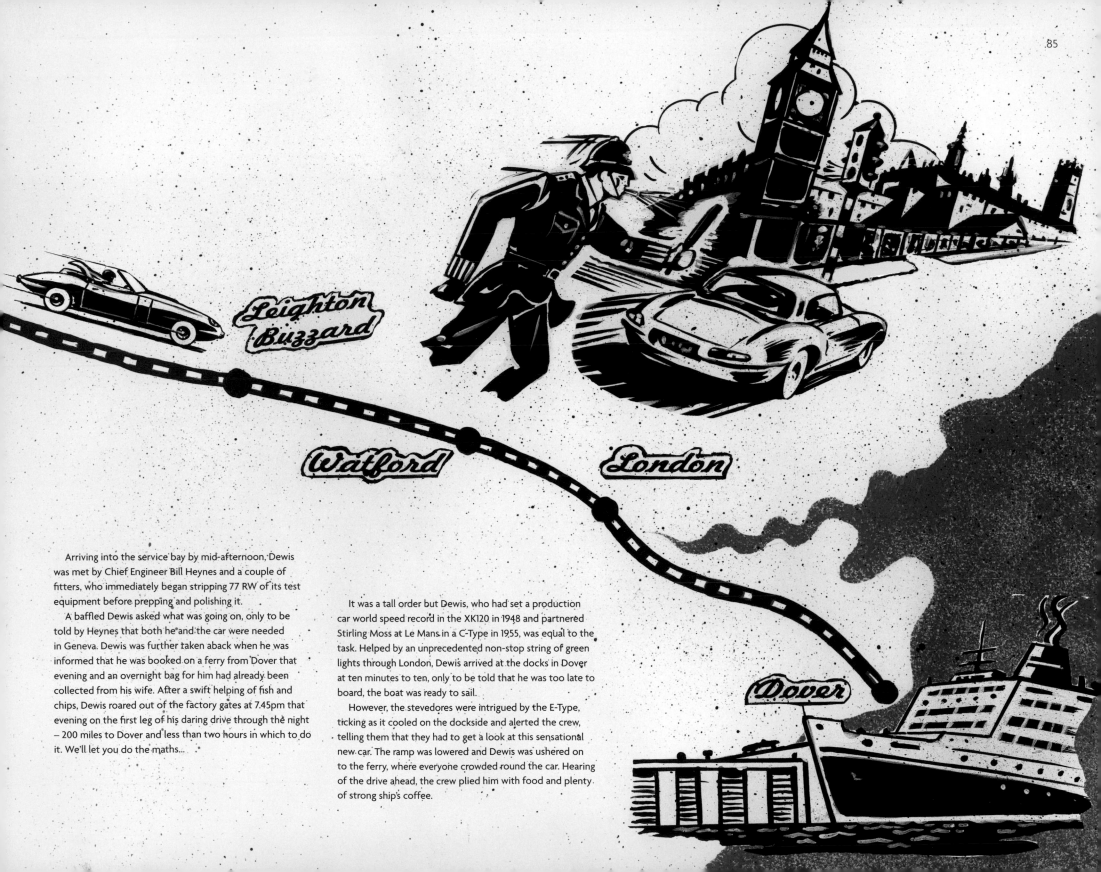

Leighton Buzzard

Watford

London

Dover

Arriving into the service bay by mid-afternoon, Dewis was met by Chief Engineer Bill Heynes and a couple of fitters, who immediately began stripping 77 RW of its test equipment before prepping and polishing it.

A baffled Dewis asked what was going on, only to be told by Heynes that both he and the car were needed in Geneva. Dewis was further taken aback when he was informed that he was booked on a ferry from Dover that evening and an overnight bag for him had already been collected from his wife. After a swift helping of fish and chips, Dewis roared out of the factory gates at 7.45pm that evening on the first leg of his daring drive through the night – 200 miles to Dover and less than two hours in which to do it. We'll let you do the maths…

It was a tall order but Dewis, who had set a production car world speed record in the XK120 in 1948 and partnered Stirling Moss at Le Mans in a C-Type in 1955, was equal to the task. Helped by an unprecedented non-stop string of green lights through London, Dewis arrived at the docks in Dover at ten minutes to ten, only to be told that he was too late to board, the boat was ready to sail.

However, the stevedores were intrigued by the E-Type, ticking as it cooled on the dockside and alerted the crew, telling them that they had to get a look at this sensational new car. The ramp was lowered and Dewis was ushered on to the ferry, where everyone crowded round the car. Hearing of the drive ahead, the crew plied him with food and plenty of strong ship's coffee.

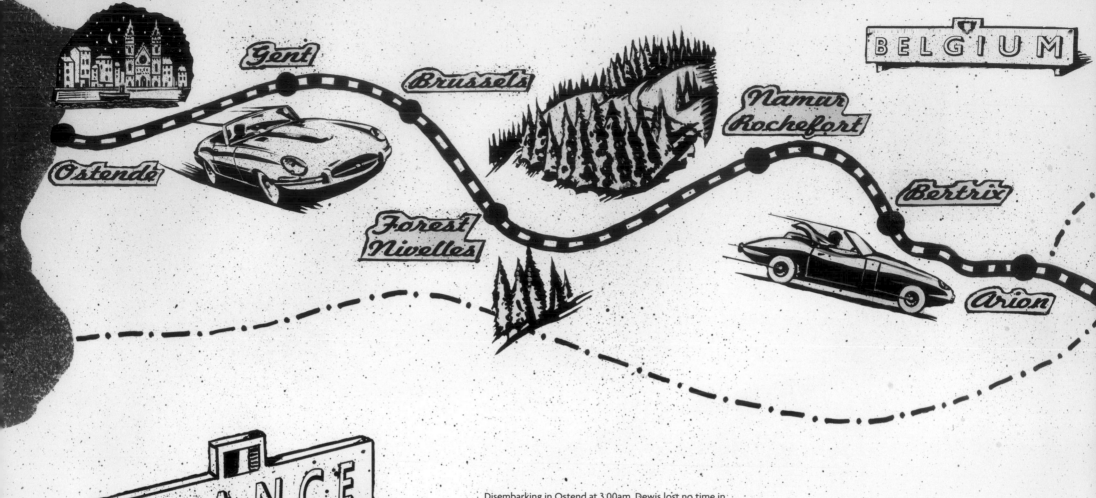

Disembarking in Ostend at 3.00am, Dewis lost no time in charging through the night. The early mists lifted and he found himself driving through a beautiful, starlit Belgium with no hint of rain, ice or snow.

It was one of those rare occasions when everything went right and Dewis stormed unhindered through France and into Switzerland to arrive at the start of the hillclimb in Geneva at 9.52am, eight minutes ahead of schedule. Sir William Lyons' only words were: "Oh, well done Dewis, you made it."

Further recognition was forthcoming from Service Director Lofty England, who smothered him in comparative praise: "You've done a good job Norman." However, Dewis's hopes of a comfortable hotel bed were dashed when England then informed him that he had to immediately start demonstrating the car to potential customers on the demanding hillclimb.

Despite his fatigue, Dewis was the fastest man up the hill, much to the chagrin of the Ferrari and Mercedes teams also running demonstration laps on the course. An informal race began, with the presence of members of the public in the passenger seat being almost forgotten. Upon climbing out, one was heard to remark to the next in line that he "wouldn't want to do that again."

Throughout the week, 9600 HP and 77 RW – both hardworking test cars rather than pampered show models – had run like clockwork and by the end of it Dewis was clearly king of the hill. So much so that on the last day, the Ferrari test drivers requested that he demonstrate his beautiful car to them.

OH, WELL DONE DEWIS, YOU MADE IT.

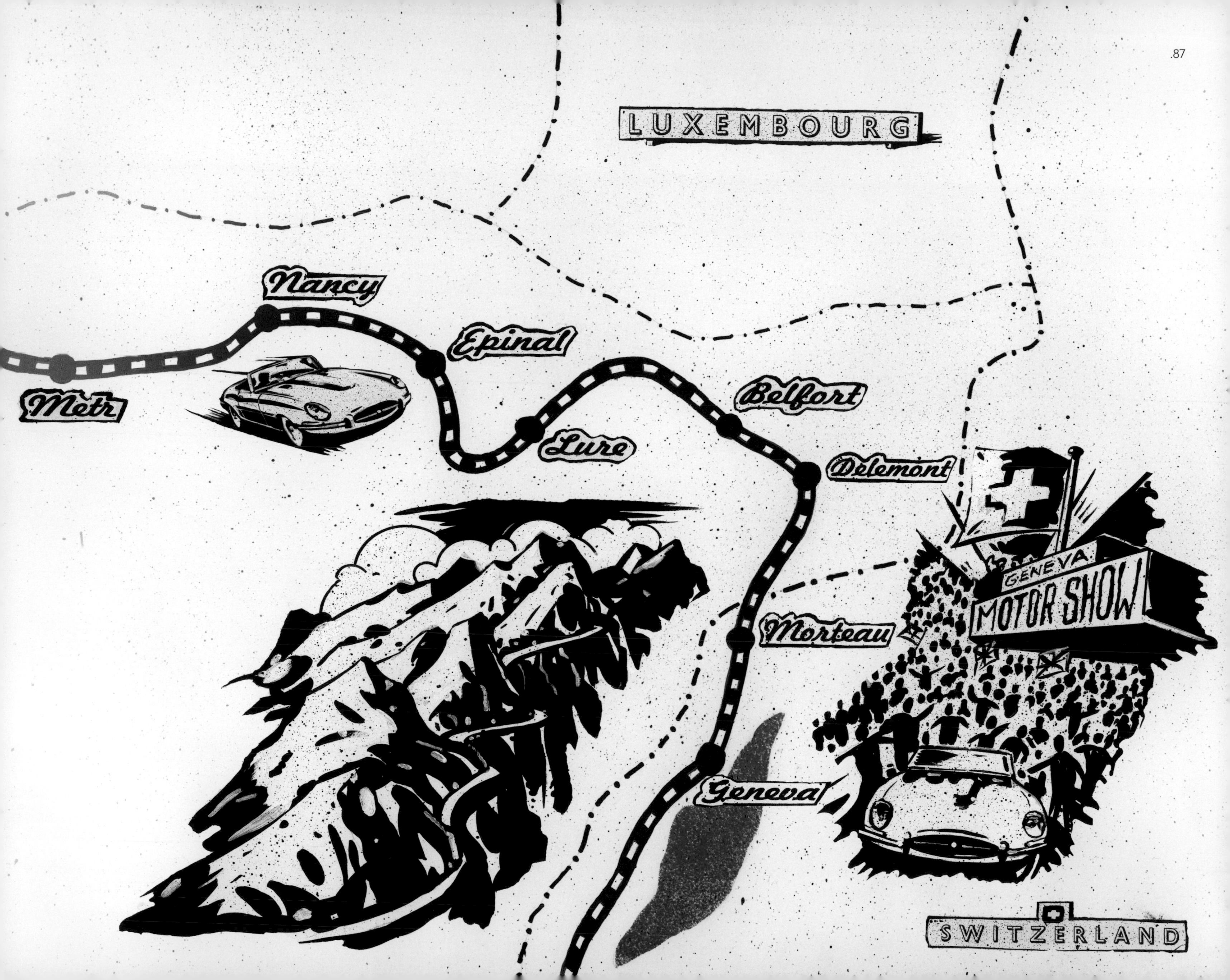
LUXEMBOURG
Nancy
Epinal
Metr
Belfort
Lure
Delemont
GENEVA
MOTOR SHOW
Morteau
Geneva
SWITZERLAND

TESTING TIMES Having pioneered the use of disc brakes in cars, Jaguar continued to take road safety very seriously

THE SEMINAL E-TYPES

EVERY E-TYPE IS
SPECIAL BUT SOME
HAVE A HISTORY
THAT MAKES THEM
QUITE UNIQUE.
HERE ARE FOUR
OF THE BEST...

· · · ·

THE PROTOTYPE

E2A

Despite failing to finish at Le Mans in 1960, the potential of E2A was clear to driver Briggs Cunningham, who returned it to the factory and had the experimental engine replaced with a stronger 3.8-litre version with modifications for race pace durability. In order to clear the larger powerplant, a bulge had to be riveted to the bonnet, a feature that would find its way onto the production cars. The car achieved some success in America driven by the likes of Bruce McLaren, Jack Brabham and Dan Gurney. Fortunately, unlike the first prototype, E1A, which was dismantled at the end of its test programme, E2A ended up in private hands for many years before being sold in 2008 for just shy of $5million.

· · · ·

THE LAUNCH CAR

---

77 RW

This roadster is arguably the hardest worked E-Type in existence. A pre-production car, it underwent rigorous evaluation over many thousands of miles in the hands of Jaguar's chief test driver Norman Dewis. However, with the world's press clamouring to drive the E-Type after its launch, 77 RW was handed over to *The Motor* magazine, whose hardy journalists had waited up all night to snatch the keys from Dewis as the Geneva Motor Show came to a close. Obviously proud of getting their hands on the first E-Type roadster, the pair subjected it to a 2,859-mile road test, praising the car for its acceleration, which was twice that of the average family saloon of the time, the ride comfort provided by the all-new independent rear suspension and its race-bred handling.

• • • •

THE LIGHTWEIGHT

---

86 PJ

Although Jaguar had officially withdrawn from racing in the 1960s, it did build 12 'Lightweight' E-types for competition customers. Regarded as the most original Lightweight now in existence, 86 PJ was originally supplied to team owner CT "Tommy" Atkins. Finished in Roy Salvadori's bespoke green racing colour, the car was campaigned in the 1963 season by the Anglo-Italian driver and his team mate Roger Mac. Its best result was a third place at the Silverstone TT, around which track it also grabbed the GT class lap record. The car was sold to Formula 1 photographer Guy Griffiths, who was embarking on a project to save the sports racing cars of the era from being ignominiously scrapped and which would later become the Historic Sports Car Club.

THE END OF AN ERA

HDU 555N

By the end of its production run the E-Type was no longer seen to be sexy; sharp Seventies creases were more desirable than sensual Sixties curves. Production of the E-Type officially ended in June 1974 but Jaguar actually failed to sell the last few examples until the following year. Even so, the company management recognised that the passing of the E-Type represented the end of an era; the final 50 cars carried a plaque bearing Sir William Lyons' signature and all were finished in sombre black apart from one, the second to last, which was supplied in glorious British racing green to a favoured collector. The very last E-Type ever manufactured, HDU 555N, remains in the care of the Jaguar Heritage trust in Coventry, mere yards from where it was built.

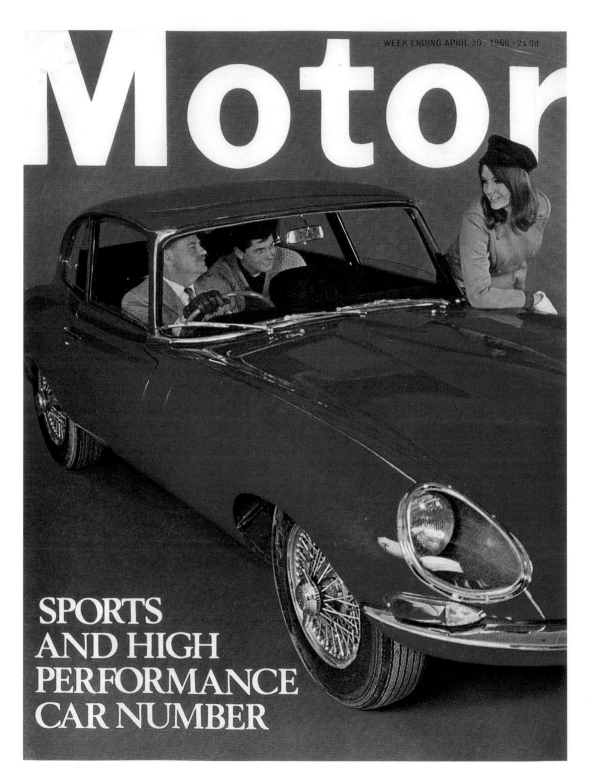

WEEK ENDING APRIL 30 · 1966 · 2s 0d

Motor

SPORTS AND HIGH PERFORMANCE CAR NUMBER

SMILE FOR THE CAMERA... Wherever you found an E-Type in its heyday – be it magazine or motor show – you could be sure there would be a pretty girl nearby

WHAT
THE
F
MEANS
TO
ME

SIR STIRLING MOSS

Jaguar has always meant a great deal to me. My first big race after the war was the Tourist Trophy in Northern Ireland, in the absolute pouring rain. I was in an XK120 and it was absolutely superb. I won, with Peter Whitehead and Leslie Johnson coming in second and third, so we took the team prize for Jaguar. I had a very good relationship with them and a couple of years later, Norman Dewis, the company's chief test driver, co-drove for me in the Mille Miglia.

The XK120 was an amazing thing coming right after the war but when the E-Type arrived, even knowing William Lyons and Bill Heynes, I was as stunned as everyone else. It was a very special car and is still just as stylish today. It is such a thoroughbred car, it has an elegance that all Jaguars share and remains with them today.

Performance per pound, the E-Type was as good as it gets and that was always Bill Lyons' secret, to offer much better value than his competitors. In fact, when I was a kid, Jaguars were known as the 'Bargain Boys' Bentleys' because they were so much cheaper than any other cars with the same sort of style and power.

Jaguar did so much for British motoring and, of course, from my point of view, motorsport. I competed in plenty of Jaguars, from the C-Type at Le Mans to the Mark VII in saloon car races but sadly never an E-Type.

The Lightweight was just emerging when I retired. It was a hell of a competitive car – still is in historics – but I think Jaguar was right not to compete officially with it. They had really set the pace with the C-Type and D-Type but the opposition had caught up by the time the E-Type came along.

You could definitely tell that racing expertise was built right into the car. One really shouldn't drive a car like that fast enough to actually enjoy it, at least not in Britain. But back in those days they were so much more relaxed about speed on the Continent. Denis Jenkinson, my co-driver on the 1955 Mille Miglia owned two E-Types and he drove them all over Europe, practically lived in the things. Not a bad way to travel really...

• • • •

Stirling Moss's career-ending crash at Goodwood in 1962 meant he never had the chance to race an E-Type but as one of Jaguar's most famous drivers he could still recognise its race-bred qualities

A RACING HERITAGE

A WINNER IN ITS
VERY FIRST RACE,
THE E-TYPE WAS
AS AT HOME ON
THE RACE TRACK
AS IT WAS ON
THE OPEN ROAD

AMERICAN DREAM Briggs Cunningham entered three cars in the 1963 Le Mans race. Two retired but Cunningham finished second in class.

The E-Type, unlike the earlier C and D-Type racers, was never designed as a competition car. Technology had moved on apace and the days in which a car could be driven to the circuit, win and be driven home again – exactly as the C-Type had done at Le Mans – were over.

That isn't to say that the E-Type's racing roots weren't readily apparent. Its central monocoque and front and rear subframes were direct developments of the all-conquering D-Type chassis, while its straight-six engine had been powering Le Mans winners for a decade.

Exactly a month after the E-Type was unveiled, two cars in virtually showroom specification – right down to the cigar lighters – were entered in a 25-lap race at Oulton Park in the hands of Graham Hill and Roy Salvadori. The Aston Martin of Innes Ireland split the pair but future F1 world champion Hill took the chequered flag on the E-Type's maiden outing. Briggs Cunningham, who had taken the E2A prototype to Le Mans in 1960, was sufficiently encouraged by this to repeat the exercise with the real thing, finishing a credible fourth in the 1962 race in a coupé, while a roadster fitted with an aerodynamic hardtop followed him home in fifth.

Despite this initial success, Jaguar was not to be drawn into running a full E-Type racing team, as it was concentrating its efforts on developing the mid-engined V12 XJ13 for a full-bore return to Le Mans. The company was, however, prepared to investigate the possibility of creating a competition E-Type for others to campaign.

WINNERS

Top: E-Types lead in its first ever race
Bottom: CUT 7, the Low Drag Coupé

A SHOWROOM SPEC CAR - DOWN TO THE CIGAR LIGHTER - WON THE E-TYPE'S FIRST EVER RACE

SO WORRIED WAS FERRARI HE ORDERED WORK TO BEGIN ON THE 250 GTO

The first of these was the Low Drag Coupé, better known by the registration it wore when racing in the hands of Dick Protheroe – CUT 7. This had started out as an exercise in creating a car to compete in the GT Championship, with Malcolm Sayer designing a more slippery shell for the car, which was fashioned in aluminium to save weight and help boost the car's top speed by 20mph. To the same end the interior was stripped out and the window glass replaced with perspex, while power was boosted by adopting D-Type cylinder heads. Regulation changes consequently ruled the car out of the championship for which it had been designed and it was sold in 1963 to Protheroe, who campaigned it with some success in Britain and Europe.

Encouraged, Jaguar decided that it would create a very limited run of competition-only E-Types to be sold to favoured customers. These legendary cars, based on the Open Two-Seater but bodied in aluminium and with hard tops bolted into place became known as the 'Lightweights'. In all, 18 were scheduled for production but only a dozen built. All featured 300bhp versions of the 3.8-litre straight-six and five-speed racing gearboxes. Graham Hill again found success, winning at Snetterton, Goodwood and Silverstone in 1962 with E-Types also taking the remaining podium places in this latter race, piloted by Salvadori and Protheroe. So worried was Enzo Ferrari when the Lightweight first appeared that he ordered his company to begin work on the 250 GTO. However, the age of the specialist racer had dawned and although the Lightweights were successful, they never recaptured their illustrious forebears' multiple Le Mans-winning form.

It was on the other side of the Atlantic that the E-Type would achieve greatest success, initially in the hands of Merle Brennan, who won an astomishing 39 races out of 43 in the Sports Car Club of America's production car racing series. Greater success followed when, in Series 3 guise, the E-Type received the competition-conceived V12 from the aborted XJ13 project. Two independent teams, Huffaker Engineering in California and Bob Tullius' Group 44 in Washington were chosen to independently campaign the E-Type in the 1974 SCCA regional race series on the West and East coasts of America respectively. Huffaker took the first victory in Seattle in August and between them the cars took eight victories. The following year, after the end of E-Type production, saw Group 44 take seven victories to clinch the SCCA national championships. This, however was not to be the E-Type's Stateside swansong because as late 1980, nearly two decades after it first took to the tracks, a 4.2-litre coupé, won the SCCA National Championship for Schedule C production cars. Today both the ultra-rare Lightweights and stripped-out specials based on production cars still entertain the crowds – and their lucky drivers – in historic racing around the world.

WINNERS

Top: Bob Tullius ran the successful Group 44 racer (bottom left)
Centre: One of the 12 'lightweights'

PROTOTYPE PACE After retiring from the 1960 Le Mans, Briggs Cunningham had E2A shipped stateside where it proved more successful

AND THEY RACE ON...

It is claimed that there are now three times as many 'Lightweight' E-Types in existence as were originally built by the factory. Rather than simply a case of imitation being the sincerest form of flattery, this reflects the continued competitiveness and desirability of the car in historic racing circles. Watching them race wheel-to-wheel in anger is still as thrilling today as it was 50 years ago.

TIME FOR A CHANGE... The E2A prototype pits at Le Mans in 1960 to allow drivers Dan Gurney and Walt Hansgen to take their stints at the wheel

THE E-TYPE
AS ART

Few would argue that Malcolm Sayer elevated the science of car design into an art form when he penned the E-Type but if proof were needed, it came in 1996, when a 1963 opalescent blue example was donated by Jaguar to the Museum of Modern Art in New York. According to the curators, the E-Type had long been on their wish-list and was displayed alongside images of its C-Type and D-Type forebears and original engineering drawings to highlight Sayer's aerodynamic expertise.

Chief Curator at the time, Terence Riley said of the exhibit: "Because of the E-Type's beauty and sculptural quality, its functionality, and its seminal impact on overall car design, it perfectly suits the criteria of a landmark design object."

Deputy Curator Christopher Mount added: "Rarely has a car inspired the kind of passion in both car enthusiasts and the general public that the Jaguar E-Type has. Even today, the E-Type is considered an icon of the post-war British sports car."

The E-Type is now on permanent display at MOMA.

BODY ORDINATES.

16	18	20	22	24	26	28	30	MAX WIDTH
0.74	21.42	21.96	22.34	22.48	22.18	20.7	—	29
4.05	24.56	25	25.54	[25:-25.6	29:-23.65]			
6.05	26.5	27.00	27.34	27.6	27.75	27.2	23.5	30
6.3	26.4	27.05	27.6	27.95	28.04	27.52		
6.86	26.74	27.05	27.4	27.8	27.94	27.5		
7.45	26.96		27.2	27.45	27.5	27		
7.68	27.0		26.75	26.9	26.85	26.2		
				26.4	26.3			

WHAT THEY SAID: THE GREAT E-TYPE REVIEWS

The sheer elegance of line which Jaguar seems able to produce by total disregard for fashion trends is allied to a combination of performance, handling and refinement that has never been equalled at the price, very seldom surpassed at any price... Here is a car which, like a pedigree gun or a green-heart trout rod, is so worth learning to use properly.

THE MOTOR, MARCH 1961

SENSATIONAL

is the word for this Coventry cat. If a new car ever created greater excitement around our office than the new XKE, we can't remember it. The car comes up to, and exceeds, all our expectations.

ROAD AND TRACK, SEPTEMBER 1961

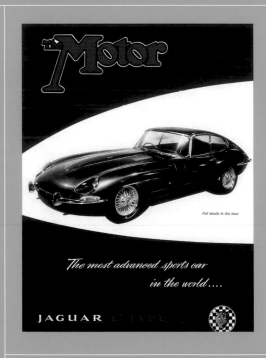

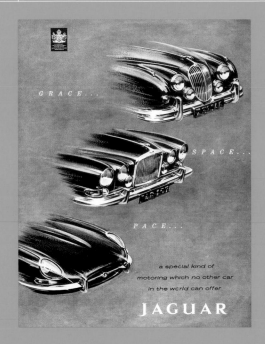

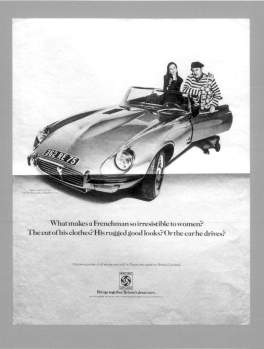

IT IS ONE OF THE QUIETEST AND MOST FLEXIBLE CARS ON THE MARKET, CAPABLE OF WHISPERING ALONG AT 10MPH OR LEAPING TO 150MPH ON THE MEREST DEPRESSION OF THE PEDAL... YET IT HAS A SHEER BEAUTY OF LINE WHICH EASILY BEATS THE ITALIANS AT THEIR OWN GAME.

AUTOSPORT, MARCH 1961

THIS JAGUAR ROADSTER IS UNIQUE

Its performance, ex-works price, steering, roadholding, tractability, economy, comfort and good looks may be matched by other sports or GT cars but not one of them has the lot.

THE AUTOCAR, OCTOBER 1967

Jaguar 'E' Type range Series 2

10 JUNE 1966   2s 0d

Autocar

Jaguar E-type 2+2 · Continental Road Test
INDIANAPOLIS 500 FULL STORY

A NEW BRITISH GRAND TOURING JAGUAR THAT IS ABOUT AS FAST AS THEY COME, IMMENSELY ACCELERATIVE, ENDOWED WITH EXTREMELY GOOD ROADHOLDING, HANDLING AND BRAKING CHARACTERISTICS AND ABLE TO BE DRIVEN BY GRANDMA AT 15MPH OR LESS IN TOP GEAR.

MOTOR SPORT. MAY 1962

IT'S LIKE THAT WOMAN YOU USED TO LOVE, THE ONE YOU'D NEVER WASTE ANOTHER MINUTE ON. YOU CAN AVOID HER FOR MONTHS, BUT ONE NIGHT SHE CALLS AND YOU'D CRAWL NAKED ACROSS THREE HUNDRED YARDS OF FLAMING GASOLINE AND BROKEN BOTTLES TO GET HER... IT'S A JAGUAR. IT REEKS OF PUREST AUTOMOTIVE EROTICA.

CAR AND DRIVER, JUNE 1965

LIVING LEGEND It isn't just E-Type owners who are devoted to the cars. An army of skilled craftsmen across the globe continues to keep them in fine fettle

AN ILLUSTRATED GUIDE TO  THE E-TYPE

FROM **1957** TO **1974**

E1A PROTOTYPE
TOP SPEED: 130MPH. ENGINE: 2.4-LITRE STRAIGHT-SIX. SCRAPPED

Looking like a two-thirds scale model of the E-Type to come, the original all-aluminium prototype was stripped-down in the extreme, lacking even headlights. However, Peter Jennings of *The Motor* described it as a "potential world beater".

Engine: 2483cc, six-cylinder, in-line; twin SU carburettors; 120bhp @ 5750rpm; 143lb ft @ 2000rpm

Chassis: aluminium monocoque; wishbone and coil spring independent front suspension; experimental independent rear suspension

Dimensions: Length 432cm; width 160cm; weight 812kg

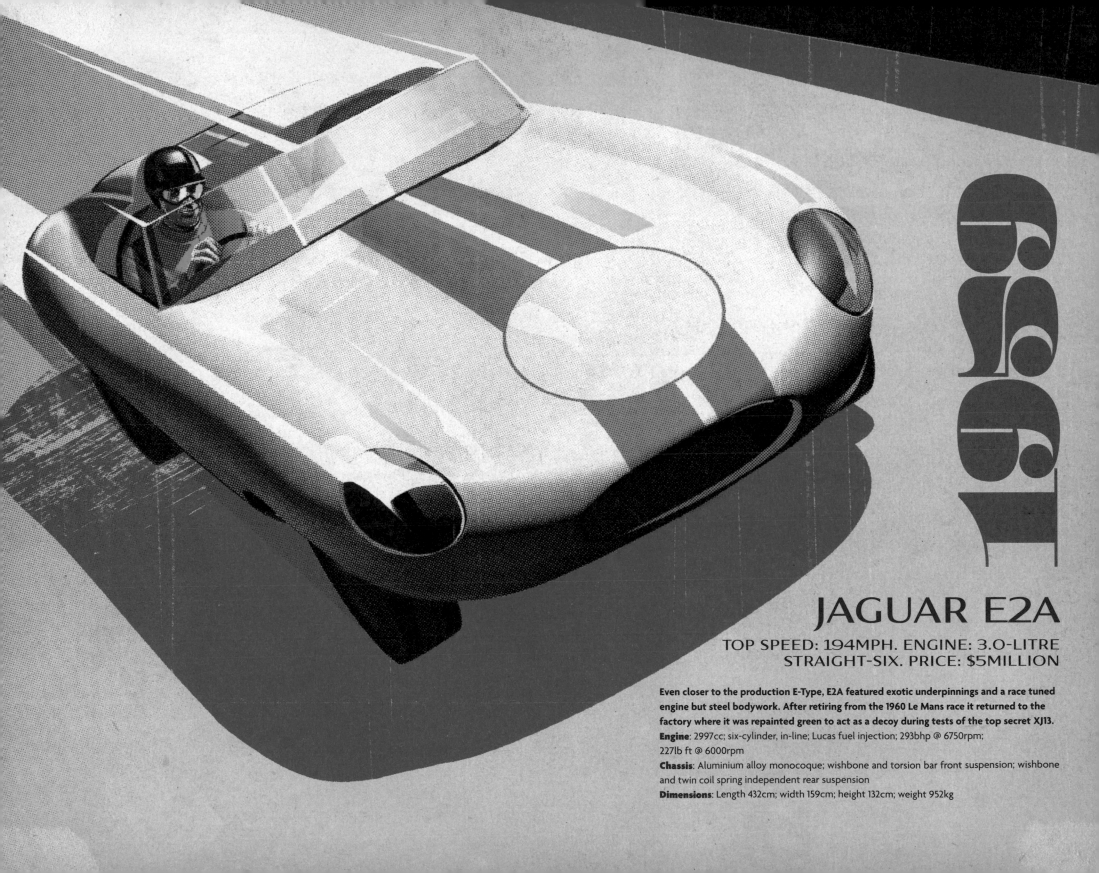

1959

JAGUAR E2A

TOP SPEED: 194MPH. ENGINE: 3.0-LITRE
STRAIGHT-SIX. PRICE: $5MILLION

Even closer to the production E-Type, E2A featured exotic underpinnings and a race tuned
engine but steel bodywork. After retiring from the 1960 Le Mans race it returned to the
factory where it was repainted green to act as a decoy during tests of the top secret XJ13.
Engine: 2997cc; six-cylinder, in-line; Lucas fuel injection; 293bhp @ 6750rpm;
227lb ft @ 6000rpm
Chassis: Aluminium alloy monocoque; wishbone and torsion bar front suspension; wishbone
and twin coil spring independent rear suspension
Dimensions: Length 432cm; width 159cm; height 132cm; weight 952kg

1961

SERIES 1
OPEN TWO-SEATER

TOP SPEED: 149MPH. 0-60: 7 SECONDS. ENGINE: 3.8-LITRE STRAIGHT-SIX. PRICE: £2098

From Coventry to the Côte d'Azur, the E-Type made any journey impossibly glamorous
and yet remained within the reach of the newly emerging, and aspiring, middle classes.
Engine: 3781cc, six-cylinder, in-line; triple SU carburettors; 265bhp @ 5500rpm; 256lb ft @ 4000rpm
Chassis: Steel monocoque, torsion bar and wishbone independent front suspension;
independent rear suspension with lower wishbone and upper driveshaft link
Dimensions: Length 444cm; width 165cm; height 119cm; weight 1206kg

SERIES 1 FIXED HEAD COUPE

TOP SPEED: 151MPH. 0-60: 7 SECONDS
ENGINE: 3.8-LITRE STRAIGHT-SIX. PRICE: £2197

The more slippery shape of the coupé allowed the E-Type to hit the magical 150mph mark and lay claim to the title of world's fastest production car.

Engine: 3781cc, six-cylinder, in-line; triple SU carburettors 265bhp @ 5500rpm; 256lb ft @ 4000rpm

Chassis: Steel monocoque, torsion bar and wishbone independent front suspension; independent rear suspension with lower wishbone and upper driveshaft link

Dimensions: Length 444cm; width 165cm; height 122cm; weight 1219kg

1961

1968

LIGHTWEIGHT
E-TYPE

TOP SPEED: 170MPH. 0-60: 5 SECONDS
ENGINE: 3.8-LITRE STRAIGHT-SIX. PRICE: £1.5M

The Lightweight E-Type has been often imitated but it was the original 12 cars which were
driven by such illustrious names as Hill, Salvadori, Protheroe, Stewart and McLaren.
Engine: 3781cc, six-cylinder, in-line; Lucas fuel injection; 350bhp @ 6800rpm; 325lb ft @ 5750rpm
Chassis: aluminium monocoque, torsion bar and wishbone independent front suspension;
independent rear suspension with lower wishbone and upper driveshaft link
Dimensions: Length 444cm; width 165cm; height 119cm; weight 975kg

1967

SERIES 1 ½ 2+2

TOP SPEED: 136MPH
0-60: 9 SECONDS
ENGINE: 4.2-LITRE STRAIGHT-SIX
PRICE: £2245

To satisfy the demands of the American market the E-Type was lengthened and made taller to create a third variant, which was – at least in theory – a four-seater. This was also the first E-Type to be offered with automatic transmission.

Engine: 4235cc; six-cylinder, in-line; triple SU carburettors; 265bhp @ 5400rpm; 280lb ft @ 4000rpm

Chassis: Steel monocoque; wishbone and torsion bar independent front suspension; independent rear suspension with lower wishbones and upper driveshaft linkage

Dimensions: Length 467cm; width 165cm; height 127cm; weight 1401kg

SERIES 2
OPEN-TWO SEATER

TOP SPEED: 151MPH. 0-60: 7 SECONDS.
ENGINE: 4.2-LITRE STRAIGHT-SIX. PRICE: £2163

1968

Bowing to increasing safety legislation and comfort demands, the Series 2 lost the sleek headlight covers and gained a larger air intake to cope with the cooling demands of air conditioning and power steering.

Engine: 4235cc; six-cylinder, in-line; triple SU carburettors; 265bhp @ 5400rpm; 280lb ft @ 4000rpm

Chassis: Steel monocoque; wishbone and torsion bar independent front suspension; independent rear suspension with lower wishbones and upper driveshaft linkage

Dimensions: Length 444cm; width 165cm; height 119cm; weight 1206kg

SERIES 3

TOP SPEED: 150MPH. 0-60: 6.5 SECONDS.
ENGINE: 5.3-LITRE V12. PRICE: £3123

The E-Type was growing old gracefully and to make sure it could still cut it against the opposition Jaguar fitted it with its new V12 that restored performance and upped refinement to such a degree that there was pressure to rename it the 'F-Type'.

Engine: 5343cc; 12-cylinder, Vee formation, Zenith-Stromberg carburettors; 276bhp@5850rpm; 300lb ft@3600rpm

Chassis: Steel monocoque, torsion bar and wishbone independent front suspension; independent rear suspension with lower wishbone and upper driveshaft link

Engine: Length 468cm; Width 168cm; height 122cm; weight 1515kg

Illustrations by Tavis Coburn

It has never been easy to capture the essence of the E-Type in words and pictures, but we hope that this book reflects the passion and reverence with which we hold the model here at Jaguar.

This iconic car is more than simply a museum piece. It remains a potent symbol of what every Jaguar should be, now and far beyond the next 50 years.

The E-Type's combination of power, sensuous styling, innovation and attainability are hallmarks of every car in the current Jaguar range. Those same principles continue to guide our design and engineering teams.

This book has been a celebration of arguably the most beautiful, most famous car ever created, but to think of it as the greatest Jaguar ever would be incorrect. That will always be the one we have yet to build...

JAGUAR CARS, COVENTRY, ENGLAND

ACKNOWLEDGEMENTS

Jaguar E-Type: Fifty Years of a Design Icon – commissioned by the Public Relations department of Jaguar Cars Ltd.

Copyright © 2011 Jaguar Cars Ltd.

All archive photos and artwork courtesy of Jaguar Heritage and © 2011 Jaguar Cars Ltd. All rights reserved.

No part of this book may be used or reproduced in any manner whatsoever without written permission. While we strive for utmost precision, we cannot be held responsible for inaccuracies.

Jaguar E-Type: Fifty Years of a Design Icon
First published by FP Creative Ltd – www.fpcreative.com

Published in 2011 by
FP Creative Ltd
8 Vine Yard
London SE1 1QL

ISBN: 978-0-9568013-0-2

Printed in England

WWW.JAGUAR.COM / WWW.MEDIA.JAGUAR.COM

Special thanks to Tony O'Keeffe, Karam Ram and Anders Clausager at Jaguar Heritage, Martin Brundle, Sir Jackie Stewart, Sir Stirling Moss, Jay Leno, Peter Holmes, Russell Day.

mance, all of which are the hallmarks of this, the world's most outstanding G.T. car. The 4.2 litre 'XK' engine is fitted as standard to all 'E' type models and provides outstanding acceleration and flexibility of performance throughout its very wide speed range. Each model features rich upholstery, fitted carpets, extensive safety padding, comprehensive instrumentation and fresh air heating and ventilation. Each model combines outstanding handling with the luxury of saloon car comfort — a special kind of motoring which no other car in the world can offer.

ALTERNATOR gives greatly increased current supply over wide range of engine speeds, ensuring adequate current supply—even with city driving—for the extensive electrical service embodied.

PRE-ENGAGED STARTER facilitates starting under conditions of extreme cold.

SHAPED SEATING designed for maximum comfort, and upholstered in finest quality Vaumol leather over Dunlopillo foam rubber cushions.

E
, twin overhead cam-
sign of race-proved 3
XK engine, five times
gives higher torque for
on and flexibility.

EARBOX
hro crash-proof trans-
oth, rapid changes.
utch gives lighter pedal
e.

r effort and greater
s on all four wheels.
for front and rear

JAGUAR
Grace...Space...Pace

JAGUAR XK-E

HE 4·2 LITRE 'E' TYPE JAGUAR

The Jaguar 'E' type is a unique combination of graceful styling, luxurious interiors, smooth unobtrusive high performance, all of which are the hallmarks of this, the world's most outstanding G.T. car. The 4.2 litre 'XK' engine is fitted as standard to all 'E' type models and provides outstanding acceleration and flexibility of performance throughout its very wide speed range. Each model features rich upholstery, fitted carpets, extensive safety padding, comprehensive instrumentation and fresh air heating and ventilation. Each model combines outstanding handling with the luxury of saloon car comfort — a special kind of motoring which no other car in the world can offer.

NE

r, twin overhead cam-
sign of race-proved 3
XK engine, five times
gives higher torque for
on and flexibility.

ALTERNATOR gives greatly increased current supply over wide range of engine speeds, ensuring adequate current supply—even with city driving—for the extensive electrical service embodied.

PRE-ENGAGED STARTER facilitates starting under conditions of extreme cold.

SHAPED SEATING designed for maximum comfort, and upholstered in finest quality Vaumol leather over Dunlopillo foam rubber cushions.

GEARBOX

chro crash-proof trans-
ooth, rapid changes.
lutch gives lighter pedal
fe.

NEW ALL SYNCHROMESH GEARBOX
Four-speed all synchro crash-proof transmission gives smooth, rapid changes. New diaphragm spring clutch gives lighter pedal pressure and long life.

NEW EFFORTLESS BRAKING
New brake servo gives lower effort and greater power for the disc brakes on all four wheels. Separate fluid systems for front and rear give added safety.

JA